Cantatas for One and Two Voices

Recent Researches in Music

A-R Editions publishes seven series of critical editions, spanning the history of Western music, American music, and oral traditions.

Recent Researches in the Music of the Middle Ages and Early Renaissance
    Charles M. Atkinson, general editor

Recent Researches in the Music of the Renaissance
    James Haar, general editor

Recent Researches in the Music of the Baroque Era
    Steven Saunders, general editor

Recent Researches in the Music of the Classical Era
    Neal Zaslaw, general editor

Recent Researches in the Music of the Nineteenth and Early Twentieth Centuries
    Rufus Hallmark, general editor

Recent Researches in American Music
    John M. Graziano, general editor

Recent Researches in the Oral Traditions of Music
    Philip V. Bohlman, general editor

Each edition in *Recent Researches* is devoted to works by a single composer or to a single genre. The content is chosen for its high quality and historical importance and is edited according to the scholarly standards that govern the making of all reliable editions.

For information on establishing a standing order to any of our series, or for editorial guidelines on submitting proposals, please contact:

A-R Editions, Inc.
Middleton, Wisconsin

800 736-0070 (North American book orders)
608 836-9000 (phone)
608 831-8200 (fax)
http://www.areditions.com

RECENT RESEARCHES IN THE MUSIC OF THE BAROQUE ERA, 180

Philippe Courbois

Cantatas for One and Two Voices

Cantates françoises à I et II voix (1710)
and the *Grande symphonie* Version
of *Dom Quichote* (ca. 1728)

Edited by Michele Cabrini

A-R Editions, Inc.
Middleton, Wisconsin

Performance parts are available from the publisher.

A-R Editions, Inc., Middleton, Wisconsin
© 2012 by A-R Editions, Inc.

All rights reserved. No part of this book may be reproduced or transmitted in any form by any electronic or mechanical means (including photocopying, recording, or information storage and retrieval) without permission in writing from the publisher.

The purchase of this edition does not convey the right to perform it in public, nor to make a recording of it for any purpose. Such permission must be obtained in advance from the publisher.

A-R Editions is pleased to support scholars and performers in their use of *Recent Researches* material for study or performance. Please visit our website (www.areditions.com) to apply for permission to perform, record, or otherwise reuse the material in this publication.

Printed in the United States of America

ISBN 978-0-89579-736-0
ISSN 0484-0828

♾ The paper used in this publication meets the minimum requirements of the American National Standard for Information Sciences—Permanence of Paper for Printed Library Materials, ANSI Z39.48-1992.

Contents

Acknowledgments   vii

Introduction   ix
   The Composer   ix
   Courbois's Cantatas   x
   Notes on Performance   xi
   Notes   xiv

Texts and Translations   xvii

Plates   xxvii

Cantates françoises à I et II voix
   Dedication   2

No. 1. Apollon et Daphné *(Dessus, Basse continue)*
   1. Récitatif: "Esclave nouveau de l'Amour"   3
   2. Air: "Une beauté rigoureuse"   4
   3. Récitatif: "Apollon par ces mots sous un paisible ombrage"   7
   4. Air: "Ah! permettez du moins, en ne m'évitant pas"   8
   5. Récitatif: "Mais en vain Apollon, amant infortuné"   11
   6. [Mesuré]: "Malheureux Apollon, tes talents et tes charmes"   12
   7. Air: "L'art de charmer est un mystère"   13

No. 2. Zéphire et Flore *(Dessus, Basse continue)*
   1. [Récitatif]: "Sur les bords d'un ruisseau"   16
   2. Air: "Vents, qui partagez ma puissance"   17
   3. Récitatif: "Il dit; aussitôt il ravage les bois, les coteaux, les vallons"   19
   4. Air: "Votre rival, ingrat amant"   20
   5. Récitatif: "Flore par ce reproche exprima son courroux"   22
   6. Air: "Tendre Amour, dans ton empire"   23

No. 3. L'Amant timide *(Haute-contre, Basse continue)*
   1. Récitatif: "La beauté qu'adore Philène"   26
   2. Air: "Fuyez, fuyez, nuages sombres"   27
   3. Récitatif: "Mais, c'en est fait: nuit, vous disparaissez"   28
   4. Air: "Vous qui différez la présence"   29
   5. Récitatif: "Tandis que le berger dans un bois solitaire"   31
   6. Air: "Dans le moment le plus tendre"   32

No. 4. Orphée *(Basse-taille, 2 Violons, Trompette, Basse continue)*
   1. [Récitatif]: "Ô Ciel! disait Orphée, ô disgrâce fatale!"   34
   2. [Air]: "Dieu redouté, qui régnez sur les ombres"   38
   3. Récitatif: "À ces accords mélodieux"   41
   4. Air: "Peut-on refuser la victoire"   42
   5. Récitatif: "Déjà loin des forêts du paisible Élysée"   47
   6. Air: "Ah! doit-on d'un feu trop tendre"   48

No. 5. Ariane *(Dessus, Violon, Flûte, Basse continue)*

    1. Récitatif: "Sous les arbres épais d'un paisible bocage"   52
    2. [Air]: "Ne vous réveillez pas encore"   53
    3. Récitatif: "Mais l'Amour interrompt les songes qui l'amusent"   55
    4. [Air]: "Dieu des mers, servez mon courroux"   57
    5. Récitatif: "Quel Dieu vient d'Ariane apaiser la douleur?"   62
    6. Air: "Beautés dont on trahit les charmes"   63

No. 6. Jason et Médée *(Dessus, Basse-taille, Basse continue)*

    1. [Récitatif]: "Que vois-je? c'est Médée: elle vient dans ces lieux" (Jason)   68
    2. [Duo]: "Hélas! l'Hymen éteint la flamme"   68
    3. Récitatif: "Ciel! quand d'un feu nouveau son âme est possédée" (Médée)   72
    4. Air: "Triomphez, vengeance" (Médée)   73
    5. Récitatif: "Hélas! gardez-vous bien de croire" (Jason)   74
    6. Air: "Dissipez de vaines alarmes" (Jason)   75
    7. Récitatif: "Jason, tu veux cacher ta flamme et ton effroi" (Médée, Jason)   77
    8. [Duo]: "Calmez ses/mes soupçons et ses/mes peines"   78

No. 7. Dom Quichote *(Taille, Violon, Basse continue)*

    1. Prélude   85
    2. Récitatif: "Dom Quichote, enfoncé dans la montagne noire"   86
    3. [Air]: "Loin des yeux qui m'ont fait captif"   87
    4. [Récitatif]: "Signalons sur ces monts ma flamme infortunée"   89
    5. [Air]: "Vous, qui travaillez à ma gloire"   92
    6. Récitatif: "Le fameux Chevalier de la triste figure"   94
    7. [Air]: "Mardi! faut-il pour une ingrate"   96

Dom Quichote: Cantate françoise à une voix avec grande simphonie

    1. Prélude   101
    2. Récitatif: "Dom Quichote, enfoncé dans la montagne noire"   102
    3. Air: "Loin des yeux qui m'ont fait captif"   103
    4. Récitatif: "Signalons sur ces monts ma flamme infortunée"   106
    5. Air: "Vous, qui travaillez à ma gloire"   110
    6. Récitatif: "Le fameux Chevalier de la triste figure"   115
    7. Air: "Mordi! faut-il pour une ingrate"   116

Critical Report   119

    Sigla   119
    Sources   119
    Editorial Methods   120
    Critical Notes   122
    Notes   124

Acknowledgments

Support for this project was provided by a PSC-CUNY Award, jointly funded by The Professional Staff Congress and The City University of New York. I would like to thank Professor David Tunley for his encouragement and enthusiasm about this project and for answering my queries. I owe a debt of gratitude to several people who offered help along the way: Professor Mary Cyr, for offering invaluable help on issues of instrumentation and ornamentation; Professor Graham Sadler, for his fruitful exchanges with me; Professor Robert A. Green, for sharing with me his knowledge of the hurdy-gurdy; and Daniel Worden and Rémi Castonguay, for their help in fine-tuning my translations. I am also grateful to the several people, too numerous to mention, with whom I entertained fruitful exchanges at the conference "Manuscript, Edition, Production: Readying Cavalli's Opera for the Stage" (May 2009) at Yale University. Many thanks are due to the staff of the Music Department of the Bibliothèque nationale in Paris for their help in finding the sources, for granting permission to publish Courbois's cantatas, and for allowing reproduction of the facsimile plates. Finally, I would like to thank my wife, Professor Marie Louise von Glinski, for her help and moral support throughout the various stages of this project.

Introduction

The Composer

Little is known about the life of Philippe Courbois (fl. 1705–30), yet multiple entries in the *Mercure de France*, the most important official chronicle of the time, record his musical accomplishments during the late 1720s. Courbois's name appears a total of ten times in the *Mercure* between October 1725 and December 1729.[1] Two of Courbois's *airs à boire* were published in the *Mercure*, one in January 1728 and one in December 1729, and their popularity encouraged Courbois to publish a *Recueil d'airs sérieux et à boire à une et deux voix* in 1730.[2] Most other references in the *Mercure* are to his sacred music, all of which is unfortunately lost, and which was performed primarily at the Concert Spirituel.[3] That Courbois had a personal connection with the Concert Spirituel can be inferred from his presence at the funeral of Anne Danican Philidor, the founder of the concert series; the official obituary, dated 9 October 1728, mentions Courbois as a "friend of the deceased."[4] One motet, *Omnes gentes plaudite*, which involved trumpets and timpani and "whose composition and performance have received great applause," was described as "new" in the October 1725 issue and was performed five times at the Concert Spirituel.[5] The June 1726 issue of the *Mercure* mentions *Quare fremuerunt gentes*, "another new motet ... by Mr. Courtois [sic]."[6] With regard to secular music, the February 1728 issue of the *Mercure* cites a performance of an "Italian *ariette* composed by Sir Courbois, which procured much pleasure" on 23 and 28 February 1728 at the Concert Spirituel,[7] yet none of his cantatas appear in the concert programs of the Concert Français, the other important series whose programs were recorded in the *Mercure*.[8] The November 1728 issue, however, includes an advertisement for his latest edition of *Dom Quichote*:

> Mr. Courbois has just engraved the fourth edition of his cantata *Dom Quichotte*, with corrections appropriate to the words and to the music. Those who will want to have this last edition will find it at the author's lodgings, Place du Palais Royal, on the side of rue Fromenteau; at Boivin's shop, at the sign of the golden rule, rue S. Honoré; and at Le Clerc's shop, rue du Roulle.[9]

Such a detailed advertisement for a cantata print is unusual for the *Mercure*, suggesting that this particular piece enjoyed considerable popularity. Indeed, an undated engraved edition of *Dom Quichote* for high voice and small orchestra ("avec grande simphonie") preserved in the Bibliothèque nationale de France is likely to be the print in question;[10] its title page confirms the name of the publishers,[11] and it incorporates several changes to the text and the music of the version of *Dom Quichote* (for tenor voice, continuo, and obbligato instruments) published in *Cantates françoises à I et II voix*. The advertisement in the *Mercure* allows us to date this print around 1728, eighteen years after the first version of *Dom Quichote*.

Whereas in all prior issues of the *Mercure* Courbois is given the generic titles *M.* (*monsieur*) or *Sieur*, he is referred to in the November 1729 issue as "Maître de Musique à Paris," suggesting that by then he had obtained a professional position of some kind.[12] Moreover, the same issue indicates that one of his motets was performed during three different occasions "in the past month" (October 1729) at the "Messe du Roi & de la Reine," where it was "much applauded by the court, and by all those who heard it."[13] Given that a performance before the royal court was more prestigious than the Concert Spirituel, Courbois may have been moving upward in his career. After the December 1729 issue, Courbois's name no longer appears in the *Mercure*, though his collection of *airs sérieux et airs à boire* appeared the following year.

The common assertion that Courbois "was at one time *maître de musique* in the household of the Duchess of Maine" cannot be fully substantiated by the available evidence.[14] Courbois is called "M.ᵉ [Maître] de Musique" both in the *privilège* to his *Cantates françoises* of 1710 and in an entry of 3 April 1710 in the royal register of *privilèges*,[15] yet the only documentation linking Courbois to the household of Maine is the composer's dedication of his cantata book to the duchesse du Maine (see p. 2). The dedication makes it clear that the collection was a gift to the duchess rather than a commission from her, and its zealous tone is that of a young, aspiring composer keen on being noticed.

Given the duchess's enthusiastic patronage of music and the frequent musical competitions at her court of Sceaux, which attracted such figures as Jean-Baptiste Matho, the brothers Pierre and Antoine Pièche, Antoine Forqueray, Robert de Visée, René Pignon Descôteaux and his son François, Jean-Baptiste Buterne, Jean-Baptiste de La Fontaine, and Antonio Guido,[16] it is possible that Courbois was hoping to attract her attention with his cantatas. His attempt probably came too late, however, as

Jean-Joseph Mouret was officially hired at Sceaux in 1708 and received the official title of *ordinaire de la musique* in 1711.[17] Recent scholarship by Catherine Cessac on the duchess's musical patronage shows indeed that the only titled musicians at Sceaux were Mouret and Pierre Marchand (also called Jean-Pierre or Pierre-Nicolas, depending on the deeds).[18] Similarly, Matho and Mouret are the only composers mentioned by the Abbé Genest in his description of the entertainments organized by the duchess.[19] Although several other musicians are named in official documents connected with the duchess and her court,[20] Courbois's name does not appear, suggesting his attempt to be noticed by the duchess was unsuccessful.[21]

Courbois's Cantatas

Although Courbois never actually secured the patronage of the duchesse du Maine, his *Cantates françoises* achieved considerable popularity, going through four separate editions.[22] This collection contains seven cantatas on texts by Louis Fuzelier,[23] published by the composer in collaboration with Henri Foucault and engraved by Claude Roussel. Courbois seems to have been familiar with the duchess's personal taste, since several of his cantatas feature allegorical themes popular at Sceaux. Among the most notable of these was *sommeil*, a theme dear to the duchess because of her notorious insomnia. This theme receives a particularly striking treatment in *Ariane* (no. 5), where personified dreams cast a spell on Ariadne to delay her awakening and her suffering. Uncharacteristically for most *sommeil* scenes in the cantatas of the period,[24] Courbois's slumber music sounds haunting and disquieting rather than soothing: the repetitive alternating-third figure in the violin and continuo is constantly interrupted by dramatic rests and by the narrator's statements. Considering that the insomniac duchess organized late night *divertissements* called the Grandes nuits de Sceaux (1714–15),[25] the *sommeil* scene of *Ariane* can be understood as a veiled allusion to the duchess's troubled rapport with sleep. Another allegorical theme dear to the duchess—closely related to *sommeil*—was the victory of the dawning day over the night.[26] This theme dominates in *L'Amant timide* (no. 3), in which a shepherd waits impatiently for day to dawn so that he may see his beloved Sylvia. The predominance of heavyweight mythological characters in Courbois's cantatas—other titles include *Apollon et Daphné* (no. 1), *Zéphire et Flore* (no. 2), *Orphée* (no. 4), and *Jason et Médée* (no. 6)—reflects yet another favorite topic at the Grandes nuits de Sceaux.[27]

Though *Dom Quichote* (no. 7) stands apart thematically from the other cantatas in the collection, it too might have appealed to the duchess, who had a well-known taste for comedy, the burlesque, and the exotic.[28] It was one of the first French cantatas on a comic theme, preceded only by Charles-Hubert Gervais's *Psiché burlesque*, published in Amsterdam in 1709, whose overtly subversive text and musical setting kept it from actually reaching France.[29] Courbois's *Dom Quichote* is also the first known French cantata setting based on the story of Don Quixote, and predates by two years the other well-known French cantata featuring the knight of La Mancha—Jean-Baptiste Morin's *Dom Quixotte*, which was composed to a different text.[30]

Fuzelier's cantata texts are fairly typical and follow the standard formal plan established by Jean-Baptiste Rousseau, the presumed poetic inventor of the French cantata: three recitatives, each followed by an air, yielding a total of six movements.[31] Although for the most part Courbois's musical treatment follows Fuzelier's poetic plan, there are four cantatas in which the composer breaks with this pattern for dramatic or expressive effect. Indeed, Courbois's wide variety of musical responses to Fuzelier's texts betrays what David Tunley calls a "tendency to treat a considerable amount of his text as a kind of *scena*."[32] In the opening five pages of *Orphée*, for example, where Orpheus first describes the landscape of Hades and its characters and then sings his plea to Pluto, there is no mention of either recitative or air in the score. Instead, Courbois employs a variety of instrumental accompaniments that allow the music to change imperceptibly between recitative, *mesuré*, and arioso, unifying the different sections with a descending scalar melody in the bass line. Courbois breaks with or modifies Fuzelier's recitative-air pattern in several other instances as well. In *Ariane*, the slumber music appears in place of the first air and is set as an extended arioso section in ABA form. *Dom Quichote* opens with an instrumental prelude, yielding a total of seven movements; moreover, the various instrumental interjections in its second recitative—depicting the wild emotional shifts of the hero—challenge the stylistic identity of this movement. Finally, both composer and poet flout the conventions of the French cantata in *Jason et Médée*, which features a total of eight movements.

The instrumentation of Courbois's cantatas is unusually varied for the period, which may further reflect his desire to impress the duchesse du Maine. While the first three cantatas in the 1710 publication are fairly typical in requiring only solo voice and continuo, the remaining four demonstrate the composer's keen interest in timbral variety. *Jason et Médée* (no 6) includes two solo voices instead of one; *Orphée* (no. 4) calls for violins and trumpet; *Ariane* (no. 5) requires violin and flute; and *Dom Quichote* (no. 7) boasts the greatest variety of instruments, requiring violin, oboe, trumpet, and hurdy-gurdy (*vielle*). The later version of *Dom Quichote* for *grande symphonie* features a larger ensemble but equally varied instrumentation, with violin, flute, bassoon, trumpet, timpani, and hurdy-gurdy.

Tunley has noted that Courbois's music exhibits "a special fondness for picturesque effects,"[33] and obbligato instruments indeed play an essential expressive role at key moments within the cantatas. In the opening movements of *Orphée*, for example, where Orpheus sings in first person, Courbois employs a variety of instrumental accompaniments that paint each moment from the description of the landscape of Hades and its characters to Orpheus's actual lament. Particularly effective is the use of a plaintive, sighing half-step figure in the violins, which echoes Orpheus's exclamations of "hélas!" in the opening recitative (mm. 8–11) and which recurs throughout the movement as the acoustic signature of his vocal powers. *Dom Quichote,* however, is by far the most unique of Courbois's cantatas in terms of instrumental characterization and dramatic treatment. Joy and despair contrast violently in the opening prelude, where rapid scales (*tirades*)—typically used in this repertoire to depict earthquakes, storms, or infernal characters—alternate with a lilting jig rhythm to portray the tempestuous emotional shifts of the Spanish hero. The second recitative also highlights Don Quixote's rapidly changing emotions with a variety of instrumental interjections and with a sudden shift in the violin part from rapid sixteenth-note scales to a plaintive, descending melody. The final movement, however, is the most imaginative: it is a burlesque, rustic air in 6/8 in which an inebriated Sancho Panza, "his mouth still full," sings in interjections and proverbs over the drone of a hurdy-gurdy. Courbois's fondness for instrumental effects also comes to the fore in *Ariane,* in which two orchestral *topoi* ubiquitous in the French cantata repertory—storm and sleep—are uniquely featured side by side.[34] Both are treated distinctively, showing Courbois's keen sense for the dramatic: the uniquely haunting quality of the slumber music (movement 2) builds up tension for Ariadne's abrupt and disorderly awakening (movement 3), which in turn leads to her storm aria (movement 4).

Much like other works of the same period, Courbois's cantatas exhibit a veritable *réunion des goûts.* On the one hand, several traits of Courbois's music betray what Tunley calls a "Gallic mind."[35] Among these are a fondness for imaginative instrumental effects, the frequent use of arioso-like sections in extended binary (ABB) or rounded binary form (ABA), predominantly syllabic text setting, frequent meter changes and shifts to *mesuré* textures in recitatives, and "gentle rocking airs."[36] Several other traits, however, demonstrate a thorough familiarity with the Italian style: the da capo form used in all the movements labeled "air," the sequential nature of the instrumental ritornellos and the bass lines, the occasional use of ground bass, and the overall daring harmonic language. *Ariane* exemplifies Courbois's use of bold harmonies to dramatic effect, involving unusual key areas (G♯ minor and major make an appearance in movement 3, mm. 14–16 and mm. 28–34), a ♭VII chord in the context of a major key (movement 3, m. 23), modal borrowing (movement 4, mm. 66–71), diminished seventh chords (movement 4, m. 34), and Neapolitan sixth chords (movement 6, m. 83). The same cantata also features tonal juxtapositions involving root movement by third, both within the same movement (movement 4, m. 40) and from one movement to the next (as in the final measures of movement 3, which lead directly into movement 4).

Notes on Performance

Vocal Scoring

Unlike most cantatas of the time, which are scored for solo high voice (dessus), Courbois's cantatas call for a wide variety of voice types. Nos. 1, 2, 5, and the *grande symphonie* version of *Dom Quichote* are for dessus, no. 3 is for haute-contre,[37] no. 7 is for taille, no. 4 is for basse-taille, and no. 6 includes two solo voice parts for dessus and basse-taille. Given that some singers of the time—especially tenors (tailles)—performed pieces originally for high voice an octave lower than written, Courbois's indication of specific voice types is somewhat unusual.[38] It may be that Courbois wished to maximize the marketability of his collection by accommodating the broadest possible range of voice types. In any case, modern-day tenors could certainly perform the cantatas for dessus an octave lower; such transposition would be in keeping with the flexible nature of cantata performance practice at this time, which tended to be driven less by concerns of specific characterization than by the availability of certain voice types for a certain venue or occasion.[39] When singing in transposition, however, performers should be aware that the transposed vocal part may occasionally fall below the continuo, in which case the latter should be adjusted accordingly.[40]

Instrumental Scoring

Like most of his contemporaries, Courbois generally does not specify which instruments should play the bass lines of his cantatas. In most cases, harpsichord or theorbo (or both) would be the most suitable harmonic instruments, though the more sustained sound of a chamber organ can also be used to good effect in movements with a high degree of dissonance (such as the *sommeil* movement of *Ariane* and the opening prelude of both versions of *Dom Quichote*). Either a bass viol or a cello can play the bass line, and there are arguments in favor of both instruments. On one hand, the bass viol was the most commonly used bowed continuo instrument in early-eighteenth-century France, and its ability to create double stops with ease makes it particularly suitable for sustaining dissonant inner parts. Moreover, Courbois's relatively frequent use of the pitches A_1 and B_1 implies the use of the French bass viol with a seventh string (A_1), a novelty ascribed to Jean Rousseau.[41] On the other hand, even in France—the last stronghold of viol playing in the first half of the eighteenth century—the cello was eventually preferred by mid-century because of its louder and more resonant sound, which carried better in the increasingly larger (and fuller) concert halls.[42] Michel Corrette wrote in 1741 that "although composers of sonatas and cantatas at the beginning of the century scored them for bass viol ... that did not prevent them from being played by the cello to great approval."[43] Ultimately, the choice of instruments was as much a matter of practicality as it was a reflection of changing tastes. Some passages feature a divided bass line, like the air "Ah! permettez du moins" in *Apollon et Daphné* (no. 1, movement 4) and the musical depiction of the *tempête* in *Ariane* (no. 5, movement 4, mm. 50–64); Courbois does not specify instrumentation in these cases, but it is usually evident from the writing which of the two lines is more suitable for a harmonic instrument and which for a bowed instrument.[44]

While most of Courbois's cantatas are for voice and continuo alone, three (nos. 4, 5, and 7) call for obbligato instruments. The violin is used by far the most often. Even when Courbois does not specify an obbligato instrument—as in the storm scene in the fourth movement of *Ariane* (no. 5)—the violin can often be inferred from both the range and the idiom of the concertato part. In other cases, Courbois is quite precise in specifying instrumentation, but substitutions and doublings can be made if they are in accordance with instrumental practices of the time. For example, in the *sommeil* movement of *Ariane,* a flute could double or replace the violin, which would be in keeping with the widespread use of this instrument in slumber movements at this time.[45] The low range of the part would have a particularly haunting sound on the flute, which would nicely complement the character of this movement.

As noted above, *Dom Quichote* (no. 7) features the most varied instrumentation of Courbois's cantatas, including violin, oboe, trumpet, continuo, and an early type of hurdy-gurdy with a chanter tuned to d′ and drone strings in G and D.[46] A violin, however, could easily substitute for any of the other obbligato instruments, and other substitutions are possible as well.

The *grande symphonie* version of *Dom Quichote* constitutes a special case, requiring violins, flute, bassoon, trumpet, timpani, hurdy-gurdy (also in D/G tuning), and continuo; Courbois's carefully labeled instrumentation in this piece colors its various movements in imaginative ways. In the second recitative (movement 4), the entry of the flute in measure 32 complements the affective shift from violent agitation to plaintive sorrow.[47] The sound of five different timbres (flute, violin, voice, bassoon, and continuo) colors the exquisite five-part counterpoint of the first air, "Loin des yeux." In the second aria, "Vous qui travaillez," the sound of the trumpet and timpani parody Don Quixote's vainglory, while the earthy sound of the hurdy-gurdy accompanies Sancho Panza's good-natured ribbing in the final aria. If needed, however, other equally satisfying and successful combinations of instruments can substitute for Courbois's choices, provided that the performing group is perceptive to the character of the piece. In one recent recording by Café Zimmermann and countertenor Dominique Visse, the *grande symphonie* version of *Dom Quichote* is performed quite effectively with two violins, flutes (including baroque piccolo), cello, bass viol, lute, baroque guitar, harpsichord, and organ (the latter two continuo instruments alternate according to the musical needs of individual movements).[48] This instrumentation, combined with Visse's vocal versatility, perfectly grasps the burlesque character of the piece and forms an effective alternative to Courbois's originally specified instrumentation.

Related to the issue of alternative instrumentation is the issue of whether missing inner parts (*parties de remplissage*) need to be reconstructed for "orchestral" cantatas like *Dom Quichote*. Graham Sadler has argued in favor of such reconstructions on the grounds that such pieces bear similarities to the operatic short scores (*partitions réduites*) popular at the period.[49] However, some of the advertisements in the *Mercure de France* presented by Sadler as evidence indicate that even pieces involving a *grande symphonie* could be performed in both large- and small-scale venues.[50] Moreover, among the existing manuscript parts copied from printed cantata editions of the period, none are for inner-voice members of the violin family (*haute-contre de violon, taille de violon, quinte de violon*), nor are these instruments included in the manuscript copy of *Dom Quichote* (1710) prepared in 1718 by a certain Joubert de Corbeville.[51] Given that no evidence exists for a specific large-scale performance of *Dom Quichote*, the present edition makes no attempt to reconstruct *parties de remplissage*.

Some final remarks on instrumentation concern the potentially misleading use of the words "violon" and "violons" in cantata editions. In Courbois's 1710 collection of cantatas, certain instrumental parts bear plural labels like "violons" even for a single line (as in the first, second, and sixth movements of *Orphée* and the second and sixth movements of *Ariane*). This practice seems to imply the use of two violins on the same part, though similar labeling in many French cantata prints of this time does not appear to have this connotation.[52] Most of Courbois's cantatas can be easily and effectively performed with one instrument to a part; one exception is the opening movement of *Orphée*, where the parallel thirds and sixths in the violin part of the opening recitative imply divisi. Also potentially confusing is the use of subtitles like "à voix seule et un violon" (for solo voice and one violin), even in cantatas with more varied instrumentation like *Orphée, Ariane,* and *Dom Quichote*, which may have had to do with marketability; as Sadler argues, "if the commercial appeal of a publication was as wide as possible," it could help the composer recover the initial high costs of publication.[53]

Meter, Tempo, and Rhythm

The meter in Courbois's recitatives—as in many other cantata recitatives of his time—fluctuates frequently, confirming Tunley's observation that much of this repertory is influenced by contemporary French operatic recitative.[54] Much has been published on the subject of meter changes in this repertoire; one particularly thorny question concerning the possible difference in tempo between **2** and ¢ still remains essentially unanswered due to the lack of consensus in French music treatises of the time.[55] These meters do not always imply different tempos in Courbois's cantatas. Indeed, for the most part, Courbois seems to employ them interchangeably, although ¢ appears slightly more often than **2** at the beginning of recitatives. More useful to the performer are Courbois's frequent tempo labels, especially in the recitatives, where they are helpful in distinguishing changes of affect; he also uses the indication *mesuré* to indicate a return to strict tempo after a rhythmically free recitative section.

In the 1710 collection, ¢, **2**, and $\frac{3}{2}$ are the meters most commonly used in recitatives; since all these meters use the half note as the main beat, the transition from one to the other is fairly straightforward. This is not always the case, however, in the *grande symphonie* version of *Dom Quichote*. Its fourth movement, the accompanied recitative "Signalons sur ces monts," features several abrupt shifts of tempo and meter—usually between slow sections in C or ¢ and fast sections in **2**, always in conjunction with an appropriate tempo label—that highlight the protagonist's volatile emotional state. A particularly poignant shift from **3** to **₡**, with no tempo marking, occurs at the beginning of the opening recitative, between the first and second halves of the first line of text (mm. 2–3); it seems to indicate a sudden slowing of the tempo on the words "La faisait retentir de ses cris douloureux" (made it [i.e., the mountain] resound with his painful cries). Notably, in the 1710 version of the same cantata, Courbois does not indicate such metrical shifts for the same music, relying only on tempo labels and on the performer's general understanding of the music to produce the intended effect. In general, in the 1710 collection, **3** is used only in arias, whereas $\frac{3}{2}$ appears only in recitatives or arioso-like sections; **C** is employed in both.

One particularly expressive use of meter appears in the aria "Votre rival" in *Zéphire et Flore* (no. 2). Here, the compound triple meter of the continuo part ($\frac{3}{9}$ in the source, replaced in this edition by the modern equivalent $\frac{9}{8}$) is juxtaposed with the simple triple meter of the vocal part (**3**). The main question for the performer in this movement is how strictly to interpret the effect of duple against triple subdivision. Given the unusual specificity of Courbois's metrical indications, it is unlikely that he intended the duple subdivision of the vocal part to be assimilated to the prevailing triple subdivision of the continuo part; in the editor's opinion, the performer should thus accentuate the clash between the two meters rather than attempting to soften their tension.

The use of *notes inégales* (the French baroque practice of performing notes of equal value as unequal by lengthening the first and by shortening the second in a series) is appropriate in many passages in Courbois's cantatas, especially those featuring much motion in eighth or sixteenth notes.[56] In the interest of avoiding an overly prescriptive approach, however, no attempt has been made to distinguish such passages in the edition.

Ornamentation

In most French cantatas of the period, very little ornamentation is actually notated, leaving most ornaments to the taste of the performer. Courbois, however, tends to notate more ornaments, with more precision, than most of his contemporaries. Besides the *tremblement*, notated by a cross (+), commonly appearing ornaments include the *coulé* (the passing appoggiatura), the *port de voix* (the appoggiatura from below), and the *chûte* (descending anticipation), all of which are indicated by small notes. More unusual, however, is Courbois's use of both a short wavy line and a cross to denote different types of trills in the vocal part of *Apollon et Daphné* (no. 1). According to Putnam Aldrich, the wavy line in such a situation typically stands for the *tremblement feint* (also called *cadence feinte*), while the cross stands for any other type of trill.[57] Michel Pignolet de Montéclair gives a complete definition of the *tremblement feint* in his *Principes de musique* (1736): "At first the *tremblement feint* is prepared as though one were going to perform a complete *tremblement*, but instead of trilling for a long time, only a small beat (whose pulsations are barely perceptible) is given after this preparation and at the end of the note."[58]

Courbois's use of this trill, which only occurs in *Apollon et Daphné,* also agrees with Montéclair's description of the *tremblement feint* as occurring primarily "when the sense of the words is incomplete or when the melody has not yet reached its conclusion."[59] Another ornament employed by Courbois is the *accent*, indicated by a short vertical line above a note and described by Montéclair as "a mournful exhalation or elevation of the voice practiced more often in plaintive than in tender airs . . . [in which] the sound is produced in the chest by a type of sob occurring at the end of a note of long duration or of a main note . . . this permits the scale step immediately above the accented note to be heard for an instant."[60]

One final ornamental symbol worthy of remark is a slur-like, wavy line that can appear in any of the parts. In the continuo part, these lines almost always appear in conjunction with a suspension in the bass line (usually the stepwise resolution of a $\frac{4}{2}$ chord to a first-inversion chord). This context is consistent with the *enflé* stroke in viol playing—a crescendo toward the end of a note serving to highlight a dissonance between the bass and the rest of the texture.[61] Similar wavy lines appear in other vocal and instrumental parts as well in ways that are not consistent with *enflé*. Some occur over long notes and culminate in a trill, as in *Ariane* (movement 4, mm. 25 and 44, in the violin part) and the 1710 version of *Dom Quichote* (movement 5, mm. 9–10, in the trumpet part); the one occurrence of the figure in *Jason et Médée* (movement 8, mm. 113–14, in both vocal parts) does not culminate in a trill.[62] In the final aria of both versions of *Dom Quichote*, wavy lines occur in conjunction with repeated notes in the instrumental parts; in the 1710 version of the cantata, they appear only in the bass line of the final movement, but in the *grande symphonie* version such lines appear in the hurdy-gurdy as well. In several French musical treatises of the period, both instrumental and vocal, a wavy line is used to indicate some kind of pitch oscillation, usually vibrato-based. For viol players, for example, this marking (called *pincé* by Marin Marais and *battement* by Jean Rousseau and Danoville) indicated a vibrato effect "produced by the rocking motion of two fingers pressed against each other."[63] In his flute treatise of 1735, Corrette employs the wavy line for the *flattement* or *flaté*, a vibrato technique also outlined in other flute treatises of the period: Jacques-Martin Hotteterre describes it as involving the "lowering of the pitch of a main note" and Antoine Mahaut as "a wavering of the tone which is slower than that of a trill and produces an interval narrower than a semitone."[64] In the context of vocal music, Montéclair identifies two related types of vibrato: the *flaté* and the *balancement*. He describes the *flaté* as "a type of vibrato, which the voice makes by means of several small, gentle exhalations without raising or lowering the pitch . . . on a note of long duration or on a note of repose," and notes that "this ornament produces the same effect as the vibrations imparted to a stretched string which is activated by the finger."[65] The *balancement*, "called tremolo by the Italians, produces the effect of the tremulant [stop] on the organ. To execute it well, the voice must perform several small exhalations more marked and slower than those of the *flaté*."[66] The *balancement* is essentially derived from a seventeenth-century bow stroke known as bow vibrato or tremolo, of which Sébastien de Brossard gives a complete definition in his *Dictionnaire de musique:*

> "Tremolo," or "Tremulo," is not a very good Italian word, and *Tremolante,* or *Tremante* would be better. Still one finds it used very often, either [written] in full or abbreviated "Trem," to advise those who play string instruments to make many notes on the same degree in a single stroke of the bow, as if imitating the organ tremulant. This is also notated very often for the voice. We have an excellent example of both in the [scene of the] "Tremblers" in the opera *Isis* by Monsieur de Lully.[67]

Marais explains the mechanics of this stroke as articulating "several notes in a stroke of the bow, as if they were in different strokes, and this [is done] by pressing a little the finger which touches the hair of the bow."[68] Given that both vocal and instrumental treatises in France at this time employed the same ornaments, it is not surprising that Courbois applies these ornaments to both vocal and instrumental parts.[69] Voices and strings—the viol in particular—shared ornaments easily, and the above explanations of tremolo are generally consistent with Courbois's use of the wavy line in string and vocal parts. Since the *balancement* is only idiomatic to the strings and the voice, however, the use of the wavy line in the trumpet part of *Dom Quichote* (1710 version, movement 5, mm. 9–10) might require instead a slow-type oscillation vibrato or trill that eventually turns into a faster trill, corresponding to the definition of the *flattement* or *flaté* by Hotteterre and Mahaut above.[70]

Notes

1. *Mercure de France,* October 1725, 2540; February 1726, 390; April 1726, 844; June 1726, 1466; January 1728, 200; February 1728, 387; April 1728, 856; November 1728, 2442; November 1729, 2727; and December 1729, 2919.

2. *Mercure de France,* January 1728, 200; December 1729, 2919. A chanson published in the February 1729 issue of the *Mercure* is attributed to Courbois in Répertoire International des Sources Musicales (hereafter RISM), *Einzeldrucke vor 1800,* ser. A/I/2 (Kassel: Bärenreiter, 1972), C4319.

3. On the Concert Spirituel, see Constant Pierre, *Histoire du Concert Spirituel: 1725–1790* (Paris: Société française de musicologie, 1975).

4. See Marcelle Benoit, *Musiques de cour, chapelle, chambre, écurie 1661–1733* (Paris: A. et J. Picard, 1971), 390.

5. *Mercure de France,* October 1725, 2540; and February 1726, 390. The motet was performed on All Saints' Day, October 1725; 2 February 1726; during Holy Week in April 1726; and on 17 and 19 April 1728. All translations are mine unless otherwise noted.

6. *Mercure de France,* June 1726, 1466. Courbois's last name is misspelled with a *t* twice in the *Mercure.* Since the misspelled name is always associated with the same two motets, and since there are no musicians in France by the name of "Courtois" at this time, it seems safe to assume that Courbois is meant.

7. *Mercure de France,* February 1728, 387.

8. See David Tunley, *The Eighteenth-Century French Cantata,* 2nd ed. (Oxford: Clarendon Press, 1997), 6–11 and 253–259; and Gene E. Vollen, *The French Cantata: A Survey and Thematic Catalog* (Ann Arbor: UMI Research Press, 1982), 28–37. Vollen (p. 35) infers that the *Zéphire et Flore* performed in January 1731 and in May 1733 may have been the cantata by Courbois, yet since the program mentions no composer this is impossible to determine; Louis-Nicolas Clérambault and Thomas-Louis de Bourgeois also composed cantatas on this text.

9. "Le sieur Courbois vient de faire graver la quatrième Edition de sa Cantate de *Dom Quichotte,* avec des corrections convenables dans les paroles & dans la Musique. Ceux qui voudront avoir cette dernière Edition la trouveront chez l'Auteur, Place du Palais Royal, du côté de la ruë Fromenteau, chez Boivin, à la Règle d'or, ruë S. Honoré, & chez le Clerc, ruë du Roulle." *Mercure de France,* November 1728, 2442.

10. Paris, Bibliothèque nationale de France, shelfmarks Vm7-163 and X-644 (1).

11. On the title page (see plate 5), the name of one of the publishers is misspelled as "Le Clair"; this is probably an error of the engraver. The only Leclair mentioned in Anik Devriès and François Lesure, *Dictionnaire des éditeurs de musique français* (Geneva: Minkoff, 1979), 1:170, is Louise Leclair, who was not a publisher but an engraver active in Paris under her legally acquired last name between 1730 and 1774 (prior to that, she had operated under her maiden name of Roussel from 1723 to 1730). Jean-Pantaléon Le Clerc is instead the likely candidate (discussed in ibid, 1:95–97): his address from 1728 to 1751, listed as "rue du Roule" (p. 96), matches the address on the plate. One of Le Clerc's principal engravers, however, was a certain Mme Leclair (possibly Louise; p. 97). It is possible that the engraver for *Dom Quichote* (L. Hue) confused the two.

12. *Mercure de France,* November 1729, 2727.

13. Ibid. David Tunley's assertion that in 1729 one of Courbois's masses "was sung three times before the king" should therefore be corrected. See *The New Grove Dictionary of Music and Musicians,* 2nd ed. (hereafter NG2), s.v. "Courbois, Philippe," by David Tunley.

14. NG2, "Courbois." See also Tunley, *Eighteenth-Century French Cantata,* 150.

15. See Michel Brenet, "La librairie musicale en France de 1653 à 1790, d'après les Registres de privilèges," *Sammelbände der Internationalen Musikgesellschaft* 8 (1907): 422. Courbois was given a general printing *privilège* for ten years beginning 15 March 1710 to print all his compositions.

16. These names are mentioned in the *Mercure galant,* November 1701, 234; December 1701, 423; August 1703, 289–322; September 1703, 289; and October 1704, 397. See Maurice Barthélemy, *André Campra: sa vie et son œuvre (1660–1744)* (Paris: A. et J. Picard, 1957), 20nn2–5.

17. See Catherine Cessac, "La duchesse du Maine et la musique," in *La duchesse du Maine (1676–1753): une mécène à la croisée des arts et des siècles,* ed. Catherine Cessac, Manuel Couvreur, and Fabrice Preyat (Brussels: Éditions de l'Université de Bruxelles, 2003), 100–102. See also Renée Viollier, *Jean-Joseph Mouret: le musicien des grâces, 1682–1738* (1950; repr., Geneva: Minkoff, 1976), 17–18.

18. Cessac, "Duchesse du Maine et la musique," 100–104. See also idem, *Un portrait musical de la duchesse du Maine (1676–1753)* (Versailles: Centre de musique baroque de Versailles, 2003), 38.

19. Viollier, *Jean-Joseph Mouret*, 18n.

20. These musicians include Jean-Claude Gilliers, Nicolas Bernier, François Colin de Blamont, Michel-Richard de Lalande, and Thomas-Louis de Bourgeois. See Cessac, "Duchesse du Maine et la musique," 100–103.

21. Cessac comes to a similar conclusion. Ibid., 103.

22. See "Sources" in the critical report.

23. Fuzelier (1672–1752), one of the most renowned French librettists of his time, is best known today for introducing the *ballet héroique* to the lyric stage with Colin de Blamont's *Les fêtes grecques et romaines* (1723) and Rameau's *Les Indes galantes* (1735–36). See the articles from *The New Grove Dictionary of Music and Musicians* and *The New Grove Dictionary of Opera* at *Grove Music Online* (hereafter *GMO*), Oxford Music Online (http://www.oxfordmusiconline.com), s.v. "Fuzelier, Louis," by James R. Anthony and Roger Savage. See also Amédée Marandet, *Manuscrits de la famille Favart, de Fuzelier, de Pannard et de divers auteurs du XVIIIe siècle* (Paris: E. Jorel, 1922), 55–97. Marandet notes (p. 56) that Favart's original plan to publish Fuzelier's complete works did not come to fruition.

24. On the *sommeil* trope in the French cantata, see Michele Cabrini, "Expressive Polarity: The Aesthetics of *tempête* and *sommeil* in the French Baroque Cantata" (Ph.D. diss., Princeton University, 2005), 190–274.

25. On this aspect, see Cessac, *Portrait musical*, 31–33, and Katia Béguin, "Les enjeux et les manifestations du mécénat aristocratique à l'aube du XVIIIe siècle," in *Duchesse du Maine*, esp. 23–30. On the music performed at the Grandes nuits de Sceaux, see Cessac, "Duchesse du Maine et la musique"; Viollier, *Jean-Joseph Mouret*, 17–22; and Renée Viollier, "La musique à la cour de la duchesse du Maine, de Châtenay aux Grandes nuits de Sceaux (1700–1715)," pts. 1 and 2, *Revue musicale* 20, no. 192 (1939): 96–105; no. 194 (1939): 133–38. For a good summary in English of the Grandes nuits de Sceaux and the role of the duchesse du Maine as a patron of the French cantata, see Vollen, *French Cantata*, 23–28.

26. See Cessac, "Duchesse du Maine et la musique," 106n.

27. Ibid.

28. Ibid. This cantata is also a prime example of Fuzelier's famous comic vein. Fuzelier was very much at home with comical subject matter, as demonstrated by his numerous *vaudevilles*, *intermèdes*, and operatic parodies for the theatres of St. Germain, St. Laurent (known as the Théâtres de la Foire), the Gaîté, the Opéra-comique, the Comédie Française, and the Comédie Italienne. See *GMO*, s.v. "Fuzelier." Because performances containing monologues were prohibited at the Théâtres de la Foire, Fuzelier devised the system of *les écriteaux*—large placards that contained the name of the characters and the text of the song, thus allowing the audience to sing along. See Vollen, *French Cantata*, 61, and *GMO*, s.v. "Théâtres de la Foire," by James R. Anthony.

29. *Psiché burlesque* was not included in Gervais's French publication of cantatas of 1712. See Jean-Paul C. Montagnier, "Charles-Hubert Gervais's *Psiché burlesque* and the Birth of the Comic *Cantate française*," *Journal of Musicology* 17 (1999): 538–40.

30. A facsimile edition of Morin's *Dom Quixote* is available in Jean-Baptiste Morin and Elisabeth Jacquet de La Guerre, *Cantatas*, ed. David Tunley, The Eighteenth-Century French Cantata, vol. 13 (New York: Garland, 1990), 65–83.

31. See Vollen, *French Cantata*, 63.

32. Tunley, *Eighteenth-Century French Cantata*, 150.

33. David Tunley, preface to Philippe Courbois and Thomas-Louis Bourgeois, *Cantatas*, ed. David Tunley, Eighteenth-Century French Cantata, vol. 14 (New York: Garland, 1991), xi.

34. French cantatas most typically featured either one trope or the other. See Cabrini, "Expressive Polarity." On storms in the French cantata see also Michele Cabrini, "Breaking Form Through Sound: Instrumental Aesthetics, *tempête*, and Temporality in the French Baroque Cantata," *The Journal of Musicology* 26 (2009): 327–78.

35. Tunley, *Eighteenth-Century French Cantata*, 150.

36. Ibid.

37. The haute-contre was a type of high tenor voice cultivated primarily in France. Historical evidence shows that hautes-contres rarely, if ever, made use of falsetto. See Mary Cyr, "On Performing 18th-Century Haute-Contre Roles," *Musical Times* 118 (1977): 291–95.

38. Composers often made suggestions of transposition and other performance issues in the prefaces to their cantata books. See Tunley, *Eighteenth-Century French Cantata*, 195.

39. Ibid.

40. This practice was common at the time and is discussed by Michel Corrette in his *Le parfait maître à chanter* (1758), among others. See Tunley, *Eighteenth-Century French Cantata*, 197.

41. See *GMO*, s.v. "Viol," by Ian Woodfield and Lucy Robinson, and Jean Rousseau, *Traité de la viole* (1687; repr., Geneva: Minkoff, 1975), 35–38.

42. Julie Anne Sadie, *The Bass Viol in French Baroque Chamber Music* (Ann Arbor: UMI Research Press, 1980), 4–5.

43. "Quoy que la plus part des Autheurs de Sonates et de Cantates du commencement de ce Siecle, ayent composé les basses pour les Violes . . . cela n'empêche cependant pas que le Violoncelle ne les joüe avec applaudissement . . ." Michel Corrette, preface to *Méthode théorique et pratique pour apprendre en peu de temps le violoncelle dans sa perfection* (1741; repr., Geneva: Minkoff, 1972). Translation from Tunley, *Eighteenth-Century French Cantata*, 201.

44. Sadie, *Bass Viol*, 39–42, points out eight examples of tempest scenes in French cantatas published between 1703 and 1732, all calling for two distinct bass parts: the anonymous *La France* (n.d.); Bernier, *Hipolite et Aricie* (1703); Morin, *Le naufrage d'Ulisse* (1712); Louis-Nicolas Clérambault, *Léandre et Héro* (1713) and *La Muse de l'Opéra* (1716); Louis Lemaire, *L'Été* (1724); François Bouvard, *Léandre et Héro* (1729); and Jean-Baptiste Cappus, *Sémélé ou la naissance de Bacchus* (1732).

45. The use of flutes in *sommeil* scenes dates back at least to Lully's slumber prelude in act 3, scene 4 of *Atys* (1676). Examples of this practice are too numerous to list here; for a comprehensive discussion, see Cabrini, "Expressive Polarity," 110–15 and 190–279.

46. Robert A. Green, in *The Hurdy-Gurdy in Eighteenth-Century France* (Bloomington: Indiana University Press, 1995), 85, points out that Courbois's *Dom Quichote* is the first piece in eighteenth-century France to require *vielle*. Green further points out (p. 85) that the unusually low range (d'–g") of the hurdy-gurdy in the last aria of *Dom Quichote* fits a hurdy-gurdy "in D described by [Antoine de] Terrasson with drones in G." Professor Green, in an e-mail to the editor, 29 March 2011, adds that "today this is a folk tuning called 'Bourbonnais tuning.'"

47. This movement is an example of what Rousseau called *récitatif obligé*—a recitative movement in which voice and instruments alternate as if in a dialogue. See Jean-Jacques Rousseau, *Dictionnaire de Musique* (Paris: Duchesne, 1768), s.v. "Récitatif Obligé."

48. Café Zimmermann, directed by Dominique Visse, *Dom Quichotte . . . Cantates & concertos comiques*, Alpha 151, 2009, compact disc. Besides presenting a viable alternative to Courbois's original instrumentation, this recording also demonstrates the flexibility of the bass viol, which at various points in the performance functions either as a melody instrument (substituting for the bassoon) or as a harmonic instrument (filling in continuo harmonies and substituting for the drones of the hurdy-gurdy).

49. Graham Sadler, "The 'Orchestral' French Cantata (1706–1730): Performance, Edition and Classification of a Neglected Repertory," in *Aspects of the Secular Cantata in Late Baroque Italy*, ed. Michael Talbot (Farnham, UK: Ashgate, 2009), 227–54.

50. Ibid., 239–40.

51. Joubert de Corbeville, "Dom Quichote De La Manche, Cantate VIIe, A une voix Et Un Violon, par M.ʳ Courbois," Paris, Bibliothèque nationale de France, Ms VM7-4769. Mary Cyr, in "Performing Rameau's Cantatas," *Early Music* 11 (1983): 480–89, mentions and discusses some of these extant manuscript parts. Professor Cyr, in an e-mail to the editor, 1 May 2011, notes that she has not encountered any manuscript parts containing *parties de remplissage* in the cantata repertory she has studied.

52. On this aspect of inconsistency, see Tunley, *Eighteenth-Century French Cantata*, 199, and James R. Anthony and Diran Akmajian, eds., preface to Michel Pignolet de Montéclair, *Cantatas for One and Two Voices*, Recent Researches in the Music of the Baroque Era, vols. 29–30 (Madison, Wis.: A-R Editions, 1978), xi.

53. Sadler, " 'Orchestral' French Cantata," 230.

54. See David Tunley, "The Union of Words and Music in Seventeenth-Century French Song: The Long and the Short of It," *Australian Journal of French Studies* 21 (1984): 281–307.

55. On this aspect, see Lois Rosow, "The Metrical Notation of Lully's Recitative," in *Jean-Baptiste Lully: Actes du colloque Saint-Germain-en-Laye, Heidelberg 1987*, ed. Jérôme de La Gorce and Herbert Schneider (Laaber, Germany: Laaber-Verlag, 1990), 405–22; David Tunley, "Grimarest's *Traité du Récitatif*: Glimpses of Performance Practice in Lully's Operas," *Early Music* 15 (1987): 361–64; Tunley, "Union of Words and Music," 281–307; George Houle, *Meter in Music, 1600–1800: Performance, Perception, and Notation* (Bloomington: Indiana University Press, 1987), esp. 13–19, 36–38, and 49–61; and R. Peter Wolf, "Metrical Relationships in French Recitative of the Seventeenth and Eighteenth Centuries," *Recherches sur la musique française classique* 18 (1978): 29–49. See also Claude V. Palisca, "The Recitative of Lully's *Alceste*: French Declamation or Italian Melody?," in *Studies in the History of Italian Music and Music Theory* (Oxford: Clarendon Press, 1994), 491–507; and Rémi Castonguay, "Meter Fluctuation in Jean-Baptiste Lully's Recitative" (M.A. thesis, Hunter College of the City University of New York, 2008).

56. The scholarly literature on *notes inégales* is too extensive to cite here, though the definitive source on this practice is Stephen E. Hefling, *Rhythmic Alteration in Seventeenth- and Eighteenth-Century Music: Notes Inégales and Overdotting* (New York: Schirmer Books, 1993). See also Tunley, *Eighteenth-Century French Cantata*, 211–15; and *GMO*, s.v. "Notes inégales," by David Fuller.

57. Putnam Aldrich, "The Principal Agréments of the Seventeenth and Eighteenth Centuries: A Study in Musical Ornamentation" (Ph.D. diss., Harvard University, 1942), 237. For a discussion of the French trill, see also Frederick Neumann, *Ornamentation in Baroque and Post-Baroque Music: With Special Emphasis on J. S. Bach* (Princeton: Princeton University Press, 1978), esp. 244–86.

58. "On appuye d'abord le Tremblement feint, comme si l'on avoit dessein de former un Tremblement parfait, mais aulieu de le battre longtems, on ne donne apres cet appuy, et à l'extremité de la note, qu'un petit coup de Gosier dont le battement est presqu'imperceptible." Michel Pignolet de Montéclair, *Principes de musique, divisez en quatre parties* (1736; repr., Geneva: Minkoff, 1972), 83, quoted and translated in James R. Anthony and Diran Akmajian, preface to Montéclair, *Cantatas for One and Two Voices*, xv.

59. "Le Tremblement feint se pratique quand le sens des paroles n'est pas fini, ou quand le chant n'est pas encor arrive à sa conclusion." Montéclair, *Principes de musique*, 83.

60. "L'Accent est une aspiration ou elevation douloureuse de la voix, qui se pratique plus souvent dans les airs plaintifs que dans les airs tendres . . . Il se forme dans la poitrine par une espece de sanglot, à l'extremité d'une note de longue durée, ou forte . . . en faisant un peu sentir le degré immediattem[ent] au dessus de la note accentuée." Montéclair, *Principes de musique*, 80, quoted in idem, *Cantatas for One and Two Voices*, xiv. I am grateful to Professor Mary Cyr for directing me to this passage by Montéclair.

61. See Sadie, *Bass Viol*, 107–8.

62. The wavy line in these measures of *Ariane* occurs only in the first edition of Courbois's cantata collection (see "Sources" in the critical report).

63. Quoted in *GMO*, s.v. "Ornaments, §7: French Baroque," by Kah-Ming Ng.

64. Ibid. See also Neumann, *Ornamentation in Baroque and Post-Baroque Music*, 513.

65. "Le flaté est une espece de balancement que la voix fait par plusieurs petites aspirations douces, sur une note de longue durée, ou sur une note de repos, sans en hausser ni baisser le son. Cet agrément produit le même effet que la vibration d'une corde tendüe qu'on ebranle avec le doigt . . . ." Montéclair, *Principes de musique*, 85, quoted in idem, *Cantatas for One and Two Voices*, xvi.

66. "Le Balancement, que les Italiens appellent, Tremolo, produit l'effet du tremblant de l'orgue. Pour le bien executer, il faut que la voix fasse plusieurs petites aspirations plus marquées et plus lentes que celles du Flaté." Montéclair, *Principes de musique*, 85, quoted in idem, *Cantatas for One and Two Voices*, xvi.

67. "*Tremolo*, ou *Tremulo*, n'est pas un trop bon mot Italien, & *Tremolante*, ou *Tremante* seroient bien meilleurs. Cependant l'usage fait qu'on le trouve très-souvent, ou entier, ou en abregé *Trem*. pour avertir sur tout ceux qui joüent des Instrumens à Archet de faire sur le même degré plusieurs Notes d'un seul coup d'Archet, comme pour imiter le *Tremblant* de l'Orgue. Cela se marque aussi fort souvent pour les Voix, nous avons un excellent exemple de l'un & de l'autre dans les *Trembleurs* de l'Opera d'Isis de Monsieur de Lully." Sébastien de Brossard, *Dictionnaire de musique* (1703; repr., Amsterdam: Antiqua, 1964), s.v. "Tremolo," as cited and translated in Stewart Carter, "The String Tremolo in the 17th Century," *Early Music* 19 (1991): 54 and 58–59. The reference is to the "trembling chorus" ("L'Hyver qui nous tourmente") in act IV, scene 1 of *Isis*. See also Mary Cyr, *Style and Performance for Bowed String Instruments in French Baroque Music* (Aldershot: Ashgate, forthcoming), esp. chap. 7. I am grateful to Professor Cyr for allowing me to consult her book manuscript prior to its publication.

68. Marin Marais, *Pièces de viole, second livre* (1701), quoted and translated in Carter, "The String Tremolo," 55.

69. See Tunley, *Eighteenth-Century French Cantata*, 208.

70. On the use of the trumpet in seventeenth- and eighteenth-century France, see Michel Morisset, "Étude sur la musique française pour trompette de Lully à Rameau," *Recherches sur la musique française classique* 13 (1973): 35–55.

Texts and Translations

The texts below are taken from Philippe Courbois, *Cantates françoises à I et II voix* (Paris, 1710). All texts are by Louis Fuzelier. The 1728 setting of *Dom Quichote* has essentially the same text as that of the 1710 version; a few more significant variants are noted after the texts of movements 6 and 7. Except for *Ariane* and *Dom Quichote,* both of which appear with slight variants in Jean Bachelier's *Recueil de cantates, contenant toutes celles qui se chantent dans les concerts* (The Hague, 1728), no separate literary edition of these cantata texts is known to exist (see "Sources" in the critical report).

The original French spelling of the sources has been tacitly modernized. Punctuation, typically inconsistent and lacking in the sources, has been added according to syntactical and logical meaning and modern practice. Abbreviations and ampersands have been tacitly expanded, and text underlay follows that of the principal sources unless otherwise indicated in the critical notes. The archaic use of capital letters has also been modernized, though capitals have been retained or added for proper nouns, including the personification of *Amour* (Cupid). Editorial additions to the text are enclosed in square brackets. The translations are by the editor; while literal, they aim to maintain a smooth English syntax.

No. 1. Apollon et Daphné

1. Récitatif

Esclave nouveau de l'Amour,	A recent slave to Love,
Apollon soupirait sur les bords du Pénée.	Apollo sighed on the banks of the Peneus.
Daphné, s'écriait-il, hélas ! dans quel séjour	Daphne, he cried, alas! In what abode,
Verrai-je, en vous cherchant, ma peine terminée ?	as I search for you, will I see my torment ended?
Vainqueur d'un monstre furieux,	Victorious over a raging monster,
J'insultais à l'Amour et j'outrageais sa gloire ;	I scorned Love and offended his honor;
Non ! sans les traits charmants que lui prêtent vos yeux,	No! Without the charming arrows that your eyes lend him,
Il n'eût jamais sur moi remporté la victoire.	he would have never gained victory over me.
Et toi, qui me punis de t'avoir outragé,	And you, who punish me for having offended you,
En me donnant tes fers tu te trahis toi-même,	by enchaining me you betray yourself,
Fils de Vénus, non, puisque j'aime,	Son of Venus, no, since I am in love,
Non, non, tu n'es pas bien vengé.	no, no, you have not gotten the better of me.

2. Air

Une beauté rigoureuse	An adamant beauty
Combat en vain nos désirs.	resists our desires in vain.
La flamme la moins heureuse	The least favorable flame
Donne toujours des plaisirs.	gives pleasure nonetheless.
Un amant, dans sa constance,	In his constancy, a lover
Éprouve un charme secret,	feels a secret charm,
Et l'espoir le récompense	and hope rewards him
Des maux que l'amour lui fait.	for the ills done to him by love.

3. Récitatif

Apollon par ces mots sous un paisible ombrage	Under a peaceful, shaded wood, Apollo with these words
S'efforçait de calmer ses rigoureux tourments ;	tried to soothe his harsh torments;

L'Amour l'avait conduit dans le même bocage
Où Daphné se cachait à ses empressements.
La nymphe s'y croyait ignorée et tranquille,
Mais dans tout l'univers est-il un seul asile
    Contre l'amour et les amants ?
Enfin, dit Apollon, cher objet que j'adore,
Enfin je vous revois ; me fuirez-vous encore ?

4. Air

Ah ! permettez du moins, en ne m'évitant pas,
Que mon cœur un moment doute de votre haine.
Est-il temps de me fuir, quand vos divins appas
M'accablent pour jamais d'une cruelle chaîne ?

5. Récitatif

Mais en vain Apollon, amant infortuné,
Soupire et court sur les pas de Daphné ;
La nymphe, de ses feux craignant la violence,
Vole aux rives du fleuve auteur de sa naissance.
Ô toi ! s'écria-t-elle, entends ma faible voix,
Je t'implore aujourd'hui pour la première fois,
Sage Pénée, hélas ! protège l'innocence.
    C'en est fait, il prend sa défense,
Il la change en laurier, et cet arbre nouveau
    Est son asile et son tombeau.

6. [Mesuré]

Malheureux Apollon, tes talents et tes charmes
Contre un superbe cœur sont d'inutiles armes ;
L'Amour pour te punir l'avait exprès formé,
De ses traits dangereux songeons à nous défendre.
    Ton sort fatal doit nous apprendre
Que l'on peut être aimable et n'être point aimé.

7. Air

L'art de charmer est un mystère
Qui jamais aux yeux ne paraît ;
On ne sait pas lorsqu'on doit plaire,
On voit seulement quand on plaît.

C'est en vain qu'un objet ressemble
Et la tendresse et la beauté ;
Souvent on les unit ensemble
Sans en être mieux écouté.

No. 2. Zéphire et Flore

1. [Récitatif]

Sur les bords d'un ruisseau, Flore dans son empire
    Attendait l'aimable Zéphire,
Quand un nuage sombre et d'affreux sifflements
Annoncèrent Borée à la jeune déesse ;
Aussitôt elle fuit sa jalouse tendresse
    Et trompe ses empressements.
Ah ! c'en est fait, dit-il, impitoyable Flore,
Zéphire vous enchante ; en vain je vous adore.
Vous qui suivez mes lois venez venger mon cœur,
Aquilons, punissez un rival que j'abhorre,
Faites que son supplice égale son bonheur.

Love had led him into the same grove
where Daphne was hiding from his eagerness.
There, the nymph felt calm and unnoticed,
yet in the whole universe, is there a single refuge
    from love and lovers?
At last, Apollo said, dear object of my desire,
at last I see you again; will you still flee away from me?

Ah! At least allow, by not avoiding me,
that my heart may doubt your hatred for a moment.
Is it a time to flee me when your divine charms
overwhelm me forever with a cruel chain?

Yet in vain does Apollo, ill-fated lover,
sigh and run in the footsteps of Daphne;
the nymph, fearing the violence of his fire,
flies to the banks of the river that gave birth to her.
O you, she cried, hear my feeble voice,
I implore you today for the first time,
wise Peneus, alas! Protect my innocence.
    It is done, he takes her defense,
he changes her into a laurel, and this new tree
    becomes her refuge and her tomb.

Poor Apollo, your charms and talents
are useless weapons against a disdainful heart;
Love had deliberately created it to punish you.
Let us defend ourselves from his dangerous arrows.
    Your fateful destiny must teach us
that one can be lovable yet not loved at all.

The art of charming is a mystery
that never appears to the eyes;
one does not know when one must please,
one only sees when one pleases.

In vain, an object of our desires resembles
both tenderness and beauty;
one often combines them together
without any successful results.

In her domain on the banks of a stream, Flora
    awaited the lovely Zephyr,
when a dark cloud and dreadful howlings
announced Boreas's arrival to the young goddess.
Without delay, she flees his jealous tenderness
    and confounds his advances.
Ah! It is over, he said, O merciless Flora,
Zephyr enchants you; I adore you in vain.
You who follow my laws, come and avenge my heart,
North Winds, punish a rival whom I detest;
may his suffering be equal to his happiness.

2. Air

Vents, qui partagez ma puissance,
Volez, troublez ce beau séjour ;
Que tout ressente ma vengeance,
Puisque tout trahit mon amour.

Ravagez les monts et les plaines,
Dispersez-vous, tyrans des airs,
Que ne puis-je briser mes chaînes
Ainsi que vous rompez vos fers.

3. Récitatif

Il dit ; aussitôt il ravage les bois, les coteaux, les vallons.

Pour chercher en tous lieux le rival qui l'outrage

Il vole impatient sur un épais nuage ;
Il amène avec lui les fougueux Aquilons.
À peine il disparaît qu'Amour ramène Flore ;

Les plaisirs et les jeux accompagnent ses pas.
Elle répand partout mille brillants appas
    Que les siens effacent encore.
Zéphire enfin se jette à ses genoux ;
    Que vous m'alarmez, lui dit-elle,
    Ah ! volage, d'où venez-vous ?
    Est-ce l'Amour qui vous rappelle ?

4. Air

Votre rival, ingrat amant,
Cherche plus que vous ma présence ;
Hélas ! je crains à tout moment
Son ardeur et votre inconstance.

Non, l'amour ne répond jamais
Aux vœux de ma tendresse extrême ;
Quand je vois trop ce que je hais,
Faut-il voir si peu ce que j'aime ?

5. Récitatif

Flore par ce reproche exprima son courroux ;
Mais, dans un cœur qu'Amour a blessé de ses coups,
    Que le dépit est peu durable !
Zéphire l'apaisa par ses soins les plus doux ;
Un amant qui sait plaire est rarement coupable.
Tandis que déchiré par mille vains désirs,
Borée à la fureur abandonne son âme ;
L'heureux Zéphire et l'objet de sa flamme
Se font de ses tourments mille nouveaux plaisirs.

6. Air

Tendre Amour, dans ton empire
Un cœur jaloux qui soupire
N'éprouve qu'un sort fatal.
Par ses soins et ses alarmes
Il ajoute encore des charmes
Au bonheur de son rival.

C'est en vain qu'il persévère :
Plus il s'efforce de plaire
Et moins il se fait aimer ;

O Winds that share my power,
fly, disturb this beautiful abode;
let everything feel my vengeance
since everything betrays my love.

Ravage the mountains and the plains,
go forth, O tyrants of the air;
if only I could break my chains
just as you break yours.

Says he; immediately, he ravages woods, hills, and valleys.

Searching near and far for the rival who has insulted him,

he flies hurriedly upon a thick cloud;
he brings the blustery North Winds with him.
No sooner has he disappeared than Love brings back Flora;

pleasures and games follow in her footsteps.
She radiates everywhere a thousand brilliant charms
    that her own beauty eclipses in turn.
Zephyr finally throws himself at her knees;
    How you have made me worry, she says to him.
    Ah! Fickle one, where have you been?
    Is it Love that has called you back?

Your rival, ungrateful lover,
seeks my presence more than you do.
Alas! I always fear
his passion and your fickleness.

No, love never answers
the desires of my overwhelming affection;
while I see too much of the one I hate,
must I see so little of the one I love?

With this reproach, Flora expressed her anger;
yet how short-lived is a chagrin
    in a heart that Love has wounded with his arrows!
Zephyr soothed her with his sweetest cares;
a lover who knows how to please is rarely guilty.
Whilst torn by a thousand vain desires,
Boreas abandons his soul to fury;
lucky Zephyr and the object of his passion
turn his torments into a thousand new pleasures.

Tender Love, in your empire
the sighing heart of a jealous man
can only suffer a tragic fate.
Through his cares and his worries,
he only adds more charms
to his rival's happiness.

In vain he perseveres:
the more he tries to please
the less he is loved;

Tandis que près de sa belle C'est l'amant le moins fidèle Qui la sait mieux enflammer.	yet next to his darling 'tis the least faithful lover who knows best how to inflame her.

No. 3. L'Amant timide

1. Récitatif

La beauté qu'adore Philène Avait de son bonheur fixé le cher moment ; Le berger, réveillé par cet espoir charmant, N'attend pas que le jour, qui doit finir sa peine, Annonce à l'ardeur qui l'entraîne Les plus doux plaisirs d'un amant. Il sort impatient de sa retraite obscure, L'Amour l'éclaire, en vain la nuit couvre ses yeux, Et par ces mots pressants ce berger la conjure De céder au soleil la carrière des cieux.	The beautiful girl whom Philenus adores had set a precious moment for his happiness; the shepherd, awakened by this delightful anticipation, can hardly wait for the dawning day that should end his pain to tell the ardor that animates him of a lover's delightful pleasures. He emerges impatiently from his dark retreat, Love lights his way, the night cloaks his eyes in vain, and with these urgent words, this shepherd pleads with it to yield the sky's dominion to the sun.

2. Air

Fuyez, fuyez, nuages sombres, Ô nuit, laissez régner le jour. Souffrez qu'il rende à mon amour Un bien que me cachent vos ombres. Venez embellir ce séjour, Venez, brillez, charmante aurore ; De l'aimable objet que j'adore Annoncez-moi l'heureux retour.	Take flight, ye gloomy clouds, O night, let the day reign. Let it reward my desire with a treasure your shadows conceal. Come and adorn this place, come, shine forth, charming dawn; announce the joyous return of the lovely girl I adore.

3. Récitatif

Mais, c'en est fait : nuit, vous disparaissez. Déjà le jour naissant embellit ces bocages, L'Amour y réunit les oiseaux dispersés ; Ah ! je verrai bientôt sous ces charmants ombrages La beauté qui répond à mes soins empressés.	But, it is over: night, you are disappearing. Already the dawning day shines brightly on these groves, Love reunites there the birds scattered from afar. Ah! Soon I will see in this delightful shade the beauty who shall return my eager cares.

4. Air

Vous qui différez la présence De l'aimable objet de mes vœux, Terminez mon impatience, Volez, moments trop rigoureux. Vous qui devez m'offrir Sylvie, Doux moment, comblez mon espoir. Que ne puis-je ôter de ma vie Ceux que je passe sans la voir !	You who delay the appearance of the lovely object of my desires, put an end to my impatience, fly swiftly, O moments so cruel. You who must bring me Sylvia, sweet moment, fulfill my hopes. If only I could be spared those moments I spend without seeing her!

5. Récitatif

Tandis que le berger dans un bois solitaire Par de tendres souhaits amuse sa langueur, L'Amour amène sa bergère ; Philène amoureux, sûr de plaire, Lui demande aussitôt le prix de son ardeur. Sylvie à ces transports feint son courroux sévère ; Le berger, abusé par sa fausse rigueur, En la craignant mérite sa colère, Et n'osant la ravir, perd enfin son bonheur.	While the shepherd indulges his languor with tender thoughts in a secluded wood, Love delivers him his shepherdess; Philenus, in love and sure to please, bluntly asks her to reward his ardor. At these advances, Sylvia feigns harsh anger; the shepherd, fooled by her false rebuff, in fearing her, merits her wrath, and by not daring to ravish her, forgoes his chance at happiness.

6. Air

Dans le moment le plus tendre,
Un objet prêt à se rendre
Feint toujours de résister ;
Et, victime de la gloire,
Il dispute une victoire
Qu'il ne veut pas remporter.

Amants, domptez votre crainte,
Et qu'une colère feinte
Ne trouble pas vos désirs ;
Songez, quand l'Amour vous guide,
Qu'il égare un cœur timide
Dans la route des plaisirs.

    At the most tender moment,
someone about to yield
always pretends to resist;
and, a victim of vainglory,
he strives for a victory
that he does not intend to win.

Lovers, master your fear
and let not a false wrath
thwart your desires.
Consider that when Love guides you,
he misleads a timid heart
along the path of pleasures.

No. 4. Orphée

1. [Récitatif]

Ô Ciel ! disait Orphée, ô disgrâce fatale !
    Vous mourez, Eurydice, hélas !
Attendez, je descends sur la rive infernale ;
Que ma lyre en ce jour ne m'abandonne pas.

Je vois déjà le terrible rivage
Où Mercure confond les bergers et les rois.
Caron est attendri : pour la première fois,
Il m'offre dans sa barque un facile passage,
Et Cerbère attentif, dans son antre sauvage,
Du monarque des morts trahit les dures lois.
Je vois Pluton ; Amour, viens animer ma voix.

O heavens! said Orpheus, O fatal misfortune!
    You die, Eurydice, alas!
Wait, I descend to the infernal river bank;
let my lyre not abandon me on this day.

I already see the fateful shore
where Mercury confounds shepherds and kings.
Charon is touched: for the first time,
he offers me an easy passage on his boat,
and Cerberus, vigilant in his wild den,
breaks the harsh laws of the monarch of the dead.
I see Pluto; Love, come animate my voice.

2. [Air]

Dieu redouté, qui régnez sur les ombres,
    Terminez mon funeste sort.
Je viens chercher dans vos royaumes sombres
    Ou mon Eurydice ou la mort.

O feared God, who reigns over the shadows,
    end my sad fate.
In your dark realms, I come to seek
    either my Eurydice or my own death.

3. Récitatif

    À ces accords mélodieux,
Pluton éprouve une douceur nouvelle.
Fils d'Apollon, dit-il, que la parque cruelle
    Cède à ton feu victorieux :
Il efface l'horreur de la nuit éternelle,
Eurydice avec toi peut sortir de ces lieux.
Mais, attends pour la voir qu'elle ait revu les cieux :

C'est la loi que j'impose à ton amour fidèle.
Un seul de tes regards doit la rendre au trépas,
Diffère ton bonheur pour ne la perdre pas.

    At these melodious chords,
Pluto feels a new sweetness.
Son of Apollo, he says, let cruel fate
    yield to your victorious fire.
It erases the horrors of the eternal night;
Eurydice can now leave this place with you.
But wait to see her until she has regained sight of the
    sky:
it is the law that I impose on your faithful love.
Only one of your glances can give her back to death;
delay your happiness so as not to lose her again.

4. Air

Peut-on refuser la victoire
Aux doux efforts du tendre Amour?
Il porte ses feux et sa gloire
Jusqu'au fond du sombre séjour.

On y respecte encore ses armes,
Les ombres poussent des soupirs,
Et le souvenir de ses charmes
Fait aux enfers tous leurs plaisirs.

Can one refuse victory
to the sweet efforts of tender Love?
He brings his fires and his glory
down to the depths of that dark abode.

Love's weapons are still feared,
the shadows let out sighs,
and the memory of his charms
brings every delight to the underworld.

5. Récitatif

Déjà loin des forêts du paisible Élysée,
Eurydice volait sur les traces d'Orphée ;
Mais l'amour imprudent est prêt à se trahir :
Orphée impatient veut revoir ce qu'il aime.
Tendre époux, arrêtez, vous vous perdez vous-même :
    Vous devez plutôt obéir
À la loi de Pluton qu'à votre ardeur extrême.
C'en est fait, Eurydice échappe à vos souhaits ;
La parque dans vos yeux contre elle prend des armes.
Dieux ! en la regardant, vous effacez ses charmes,
Et l'enfer à vos yeux se ferme pour jamais.

Already far from the forests of peaceful Elysium
Eurydice was tracing Orpheus's footsteps;
yet reckless love is ready to betray itself:
impatient Orpheus wants to see the one he loves again.
Tender husband, stop, you are destroying yourself!
    You should obey
Pluto's law instead of your excessive ardor.
It is over, Eurydice escapes your hold;
before your eyes, Fate takes up arms against her.
O Gods! By looking at her, you destroy her charms,
and hell closes its gates forever before your eyes.

6. Air

Ah ! doit-on d'un feu trop tendre
Écouter toujours l'ardeur ?
Lorsqu'on ne sait pas l'attendre,
On perd souvent son bonheur.

Ah! Must one always succumb to the ardor
of a too tender fire?
He who cannot make himself wait
often loses his chance at joy.

Quel est d'un cœur qui soupire
Le fatal égarement !
Il risque un bien qu'il désire
Pour l'avancer d'un moment.

How deadly is the foolishness
of a sighing heart!
It endangers the object it desires
by hurrying its arrival by a moment.

No. 5. Ariane

1. Récitatif

Sous les arbres épais d'un paisible bocage
Ariane dormait dans l'île de Naxos,
    Tandis que son amant volage
    Traversait l'empire des flots.
    Les songes, ces trompeurs aimables,
Enchantent la princesse et par de feints plaisirs
    Diffèrent des maux véritables ;
    Et dans ces instants favorables
L'Amour à la douleur dérobe ses soupirs.

Beneath the dense foliage of a peaceful grove,
Ariadne was asleep on the island of Naxos,
    while her fickle lover
    crossed the empire of the seas.
    Dreams, these delightful deceivers,
enchant the princess, and with false pleasures
    defer true suffering;
    and in these favorable moments,
Love steals away sorrow's sighs.

2. [Air]

    Ne vous réveillez pas encore,
Beaux yeux, vous ne verrez que trop tôt vos malheurs.
    Semblables à ceux de l'aurore,
Vous ne vous ouvrirez que pour verser des pleurs.

    Do not awaken yet,
lovely eyes, you will see all too soon your misfortunes.
    Like those of the dawn
you will open only to shed tears.

3. Récitatif

Mais l'Amour interrompt les songes qui l'amusent ;
Ariane s'éveille, ô funeste moment !
    Son cœur croit que ses yeux l'abusent
Et veut justifier son infidèle amant.
Tout la détrompe ; enfin elle court sur la rive,
Et son désordre expose à la clarté du jour
Des appas réservés aux regards de l'Amour.
    Les accents de sa voix plaintive
Font gémir après eux les échos d'alentour ;
    Ingrat, dit-elle, hélas ! tu fuis et je t'adore.
    Tu fuis, quel prix de mes bienfaits !
Peux-tu te souvenir du fatal Minotaure,
    Et trahir mes faibles attraits ?
Que vois-je ? le vaisseau du perfide Thésée ;
Que ce funeste objet redouble mes fureurs !
Ah ! c'en est fait, ah ! montrez, Dieux vengeurs,
Que vous êtes l'appui de la foi méprisée.

But Love interrupts the dreams that delight her.
Ariadne awakens, O fateful moment!
    Her heart believes her eyes are deceiving her,
and tries to make excuses for her unfaithful lover.
Everything deceives her; at last, she runs onto the shore,
and her disarray reveals, in the light of day,
sights reserved to Love's eyes alone.
    The accents of her plaintive voice
make echoes moan all around her.
    Ungrateful one, she says, alas! You flee and I adore you.
    You flee, a fit reward for my good deeds!
Can you recall the deadly Minotaur,
    and still betray my delicate beauty?
What do I see? The vessel of the perfidious Theseus.
May this doleful object redouble my fury!
Ah! it is done, ah! show, vengeful gods,
that you are the pillar of my spurned trust.

4. [Air]

Dieu des mers, servez mon courroux,	God of the seas, serve my wrath,
Que le ciel éclate, qu'il tonne ;	let the heavens flash with lightning, let thunder roar!
Vents furieux, conjurez tous	Fierce winds, conspire together
Contre un amant qui m'abandonne.	against a lover who forsakes me.

Frappez, du plus mortel effroi,
Le cœur d'un ingrat qui m'offense,
Faites qu'il souffre autant que moi ;
Et vous remplirez ma vengeance.

Strike the most mortal terror
into the heart of an ingrate who offends me;
make him suffer as much as I have,
and you will fulfill my vengeance.

5. Récitatif

Quel Dieu vient d'Ariane apaiser la douleur ?
De l'Inde renommé[e], c'est le fameux vainqueur.
L'Amour lui prête-t-il son arc et sa puissance ?
Quel charme surprenant, quelle prompte inconstance !
De la triste princesse il enchante le cœur,
Par un brillant hommage, il répare sa gloire
Et venge les affronts que ses yeux ont reçus ;
Du perfide Thésée elle perd la mémoire,
Et tout son cœur se livre à l'amour de Bacchus.

Which god comes to appease Ariadne's grief?
He is the famous conqueror of renowned India.
Does Love lend him his bow and his power?
What astonishing charm, what sudden inconstancy!
He captivates the heart of the unhappy princess;
in a splendid homage, he restores her glory,
and avenges the affronts that her eyes have witnessed;
she loses all memory of perfidious Theseus,
and her whole heart surrenders to the love of Bacchus.

6. Air

Beautés dont on trahit les charmes,
Et qu'un volage ose outrager,
Ne livrez pas vos yeux aux larmes ;
Qu'ils vous prêtent plutôt des armes
Pour le punir et vous venger.

O beauties, whose charms have been betrayed,
and that a fickle man dares to scorn,
do not give your eyes over to tears;
let them instead be your weapons
to punish him and get revenge.

Pour une victoire nouvelle
Préparez vos aimables traits ;
Et qu'une conquête plus belle
De la perte d'un infidèle
Dédommage vos doux attraits.

Prepare your lovely features
for a new victory;
may a more beautiful conquest
make amends with your sweet charms
for the loss of an unfaithful one.

No. 6. Jason et Médée

1. [Récitatif]

JASON
Que vois-je ? c'est Médée : elle vient dans ces lieux.
　Hélas ! que je crains qu'à ses yeux
L'amour qui la trahit ne s'accuse lui-même.
Que deviendrais-je ? ô ciel ! si ma trop vive ardeur

　Lui décelait l'objet que j'aime ;
　Feignons pour tromper sa fureur.

JASON
What do I see? It is Medea: she comes to this place.
　Alas! How I dread that, under her gaze,
the love that has betrayed her might give itself away.
What shall become of me? O heavens! What if my excessive ardor
　revealed the object of my love to her?
　Let us feign so as to deceive her fury.

2. [Duo]

JASON, MÉDÉE
Hélas ! l'Hymen éteint la flamme
Dont l'amour brûlait votre cœur ;
Je ne règne plus sur votre âme,
Vos yeux m'apprennent mon malheur.

JASON, MEDEA
Alas! Hymen has extinguished the flame
with which love burned your heart;
I no longer reign over your soul,
your eyes tell me of my misfortune.

3. Récitatif

MÉDÉE
Ciel ! quand d'un feu nouveau son âme est possédée,

　Quand Créuse a su l'engager,
　Jason m'accuse de changer.

MEDEA
Heavens! Even though his soul is possessed by a new fire,
　even though Creusa was able to win him over,
　Jason accuses me of being fickle.

xxiii

Ingrat, songes-tu bien que tu trahis Médée ?
Ne te souvient-il plus du pouvoir dangereux
Qui du séjour des morts m'ouvre les noirs abîmes ?

Perfide, en oubliant mon amour malheureux,
    As-tu donc oublié ses crimes ?
N'ont-ils pas à tes yeux assez fait éclater
    Et ma tendresse et ma puissance ?
Il n'en est pas un seul qui ne dût exciter
    Ta crainte et ta reconnaissance.

4. Air

MÉDÉE

Triomphez, vengeance,
Venez m'irriter ;
Souffrir une offense
C'est la mériter.

Que l'amour murmure,
Suivons la fureur ;
Perdons le parjure
Dont je perds le cœur.

5. Récitatif

JASON

    Hélas ! gardez-vous bien de croire
Ce que votre fureur vous inspire aujourd'hui.
La princesse défend vos jours et votre gloire,
Mon respect et mes soins vous donnent son appui,
Créon est prévenu, contre vous on l'anime ;
    Vous pourriez être sa victime
Sans le secours d'un cœur plus généreux que lui.

6. Air

JASON

Dissipez de vaines alarmes,
Et comptez plus sur vos appas
Où vous brillez ; ne craignez pas
Qu'on ravisse un cœur à vos charmes.

On ressent en vain d'autres feux,
Dès qu'on vous voit, on est volage,
Mais jamais on ne se dégage
Quand on soupire dans vos nœuds.

7. Récitatif

MÉDÉE

Jason, tu veux cacher ta flamme et ton effroi
Pour éviter ma vengeance fatale ;
    Ah ! tu trembles pour ma rivale
    Quand tu feins de trembler pour moi.

JASON

Non, Créuse à vos lois ne me rend pas rebelle :
Mon cœur par ses beaux yeux n'a pas été surpris.
    De tous les soins que j'ai pour elle,
C'est vous, hélas ! qui me devez le prix.

MÉDÉE

Ah ! contre vos soupirs je ne puis me défendre ;
    Si vous trompez mon cœur trop tendre,
    Gardez-vous de le détromper.

Ingrate, do you not know you have betrayed Medea?
Don't you remember the dangerous powers
that can open the dark abysses of the house of the dead for me?

You wretch, by forgetting my ill-fated love,
    have you then forgotten its crimes?
Have they not done enough to strike your eyes
    with both my tenderness and my power?
Any of them would have had to excite
    your fear and your gratitude.

MEDEA

Triumph, O vengeance,
come to inflame me;
to suffer an insult
is to deserve it.

Let love whisper,
let us follow rage;
let us rid ourselves of the liar
whose heart I have lost.

JASON

    Alas! Beware of believing
what your rage conjures up for you today.
The princess praises your life and your glory,
my respect and my good words assure you her support,
Creon is forewarned, he is being incensed against you;
    you could fall victim to him
without the help of a heart more valiant than he.

JASON

Dispel vain alarms,
and rely more on your charms,
where you shine; do not fear
that one might snatch a heart away from your charms.

One feels other fires in vain,
as soon as one sees you, one is fickle,
yet never does one get away
once one is caught in your web of love.

MEDEA

Jason, you are trying to hide your flame and your terror
to avoid my deadly vengeance;
    Ah! You tremble for my rival
    while you pretend to tremble for me.

JASON

No, it's not Creusa who makes me resist your laws:
my heart has not been stunned by her beautiful eyes.
    For all the respects I have paid her,
it is you, alas, who owe me a reward.

MEDEA

Ah! I cannot defend myself against your sighs;
    if you deceive my overly tender heart,
    be careful not to disabuse it.

<table>
<tr><td>

JASON
À vos transports jaloux gardez-vous de vous rendre ;
Votre cœur, s'il m'aimait, devrait les dissiper.

8. [Duo]

JASON, MÉDÉE
Calmez ses/mes soupçons et ses/mes peines,
Régnez, triomphez, tendre Amour.
Il faut que l'Hymen en ce jour
Vous ait pour garant de ses chaînes.

</td><td>

JASON
Beware of surrendering to your jealous passions;
your heart, if it really loved me, should dissipate them.

JASON, MEDEA
Assuage her/my suspicions and her/my pains;
reign, triumph, O tender Love.
On this day, Hymen must have you
as guarantor of his chains.

</td></tr>
</table>

No. 7. Dom Quichote

<table>
<tr><td>

2. Récitatif

Dom Quichote, enfoncé dans la montagne noire,
La faisait retentir de ses cris douloureux :
Achevons, disait-il, mille exploits amoureux
    Que l'avenir ne puisse croire.
Ô ! Dulcinée, ô ! toi, source de mes ennuis,
    Divine perle de la Manche,
Beau soleil de mes jours et lune de mes nuits,
Que de moments heureux ta rigueur me retranche.

3. [Air]

Loin des yeux qui m'ont fait captif,
Je brûle d'une ardeur grégeoise ;
Jamais un penser lénitif
N'allège mon âme pantoise.

Chaque jour je navre le cœur
De mainte reine languissante,
Et je préfère à leur douceur
La cruauté de mon infante.

4. [Récitatif]

Signalons sur ces monts ma flamme infortunée,
    Et les attraits de Dulcinée.
C'en est fait, égalons les efforts furieux
    Du terrible amant d'Angélique :
Désolons, ravageons cette forêt antique,
Renversons ces rochers ; mais non, je ferais mieux
D'imiter d'Amadis la douleur pacifique.
Surpassons, s'il se peut, de ce beau ténébreux
    L'incomparable pénitence :
Coulez, mes pleurs, garants de ma constance,
    Inondez ces déserts affreux.
Et vous, race félonne, à me nuire occupée,
Géants outrecuidés, perfides nécromants,
Je dépose aujourd'hui ma redoutable épée ;
Pour la première fois, goûtez de doux moments.

5. [Air]

Vous, qui travaillez à ma gloire,
Venez, volez, sage enchanteur ;
Consacrez l'illustre mémoire
Des miracles de mon ardeur.

N'oubliez pas dans mon histoire
Un seul instant de ce grand jour ;
Je vais donner à la victoire
Le repos que m'ôte l'amour.

</td><td>

Don Quixote, deep in the dark mountain,
made it resound with his painful cries:
let us achieve, said he, a thousand amorous feats
    that posterity will not believe.
O Dulcinea, O you, source of my troubles,
    divine pearl of La Mancha,
radiant sun of my days and moon of my nights,
how many happy moments does your sternness take
    from me.

Far from the eyes that have taken me captive,
I burn with a passion like Greek fire;
never does a calming thought
soothe my stunned soul.

Every day I break the heart
of many a languid queen,
and, to their sweetness, I prefer
the cruelty of my Infanta.

On these mountains, let us proclaim my wretched flame,
    and the charms of Dulcinea.
It is done, let us equal the fervent efforts
    of Angelica's fearsome lover:
let us destroy, let us ravage this ancient forest,
let us overturn these rocks; but no, I would do better
to imitate the silent suffering of Amadis.
Let us surpass, if possible, the unrivaled punishment
    of that troubled youth.
Flow, my tears, proof of my constancy,
    inundate these frightful deserts.
And you, treacherous race, keen on harming me,
insolent giants, perfidious necromancers,
today I lay down my formidable sword;
for the first time, taste sweet moments.

You who contribute to my glory,
come, fly, O wise wizard;
consecrate the illustrious memory
of the miracles of my ardor.

In my story, do not forget
a single instant of this great day;
I am going to give victory
the peace that love has denied me.

</td></tr>
</table>

6. Récitatif

Le fameux Chevalier de la triste figure	The famous knight of the sad countenance
Par ces fougueux transports insultait la raison,	defied reason with these fiery outbursts,
Tandis que Rossinante, escorté du grison,	while Rocinante, escorted by the ass,
Sur de maigres rochers dépouillés de verdure	labored to snatch an arid tuft of grass
S'efforçait d'arracher un aride gazon.	on thin rocks devoid of foliage.
Là, le sobre Sancho, secondant son courage	There, sober Sancho, stoking his courage
Par un reste de cervelas,	with some leftover sausage,
À son large flacon livrait de doux combats,	wrestled gently with his large flask,
Et goûtait à longs traits un plus charmant breuvage	and tasted, in long drafts, a brew more charming
Que le baume de Fierabras.	than the balm of Fierabras.
Mais voyant son cher maître accablé de sa peine,	But seeing his dear master overwhelmed by his own suffering,
De ses tendres chagrins entretenir les ours,	enchanting the bears with the telling of his tender troubles,
Le fidèle écuyer, la bouche encore pleine,	the faithful squire, his mouth still full,
S'essuya la moustache et lui tint ce discours.	wiped his moustache and delivered this speech.

Comment. In the 1728 setting, the sixth and seventh lines of this recitative read "Sancho, dans ce désert sauvage, / Peu touché de leur embarras" (Sancho, in this wild desert, / little bothered by their foolishness), and the final four lines read "Mais d'un maître chéri la tristesse fatale / De ses plaisirs interrompit le cours ; / Le fidèle écuyer, rappelant sa morale, / Au tendre Dom Quichot[e] adressa ce discours" (Yet the tragic sadness of his beloved master / interrupted the course of his pleasures; / the faithful squire, recalling his lesson, / addressed this speech to the tender Don Quixote).

7. [Air]

Mardi ! faut-il pour une ingrate	'Sdeath! Just for an ungrateful woman,
Passer tant de nuits sans grabat ?	must one go so many nights with no cot to sleep in?
Palsangué ! grattons qui nous gratte,	Zounds! You scratch my back, I scratch yours,
Autrement à bon chat bon rat.	otherwise, tit for tat.
Le jeu ne vaut pas la chandelle,	The game is not worth the candle,
Votre infante est une guenon ;	your Infanta is a hag;
La sauce que l'on fait pour elle	the sauce that one prepares for her
Coûte plus cher que le poisson.	costs more than the fish.

Comment. Given the burlesque context, the opening word "mardi" is probably intended as a wordplay on "mordié," a variant of the interjection "mordieu" (*Mort Dieu*). This agrees with the spelling "mordi" used in the *grande symphonie* version of this cantata. Another possibility could be a wordplay on "pardi," another interjection.

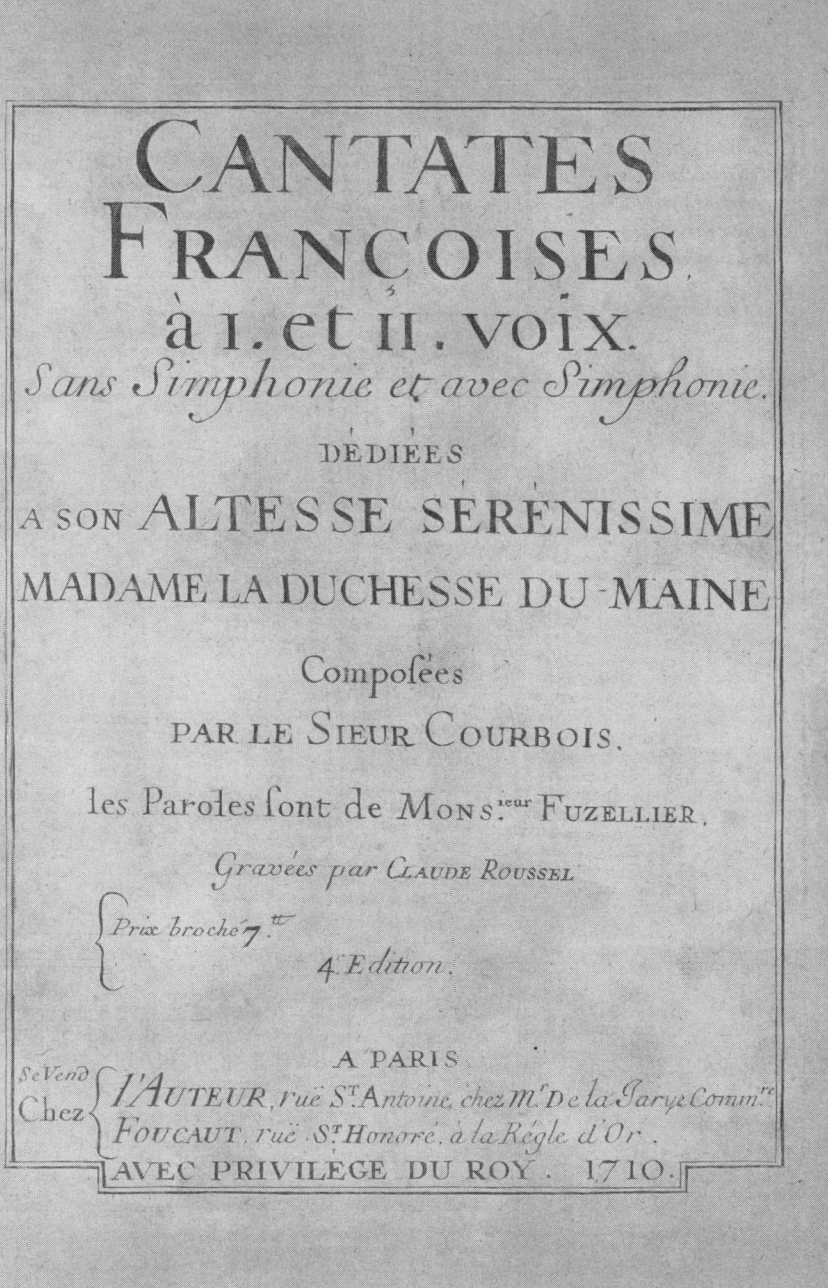

Plate 1. Philippe Courbois, *Cantates françoises à I et II voix sans simphonie et avec simphonie* (Paris: Henri Foucault, 1710), title page. Bibliothèque nationale de France, D-8466 (2). Courtesy of the Bibliothèque nationale de France.

Plate 2. Philippe Courbois, *Cantates françoises à I et II voix sans simphonie et avec simphonie* (Paris: Henri Foucault, 1710), page 1, *Apollon et Daphné*, "Esclave nouveau de l'Amour" (movement 1). Bibliothèque nationale de France, D-8466 (2). Courtesy of the Bibliothèque nationale de France.

Plate 3. Philippe Courbois, *Cantates françoises à I et II voix sans simphonie et avec simphonie* (Paris: Henri Foucault, 1710), page 33, violin divisi in *Orphée*, "Ô Ciel! disait Orphée" (movement 1). Bibliothèque nationale de France, D-8466 (2). Courtesy of the Bibliothèque nationale de France.

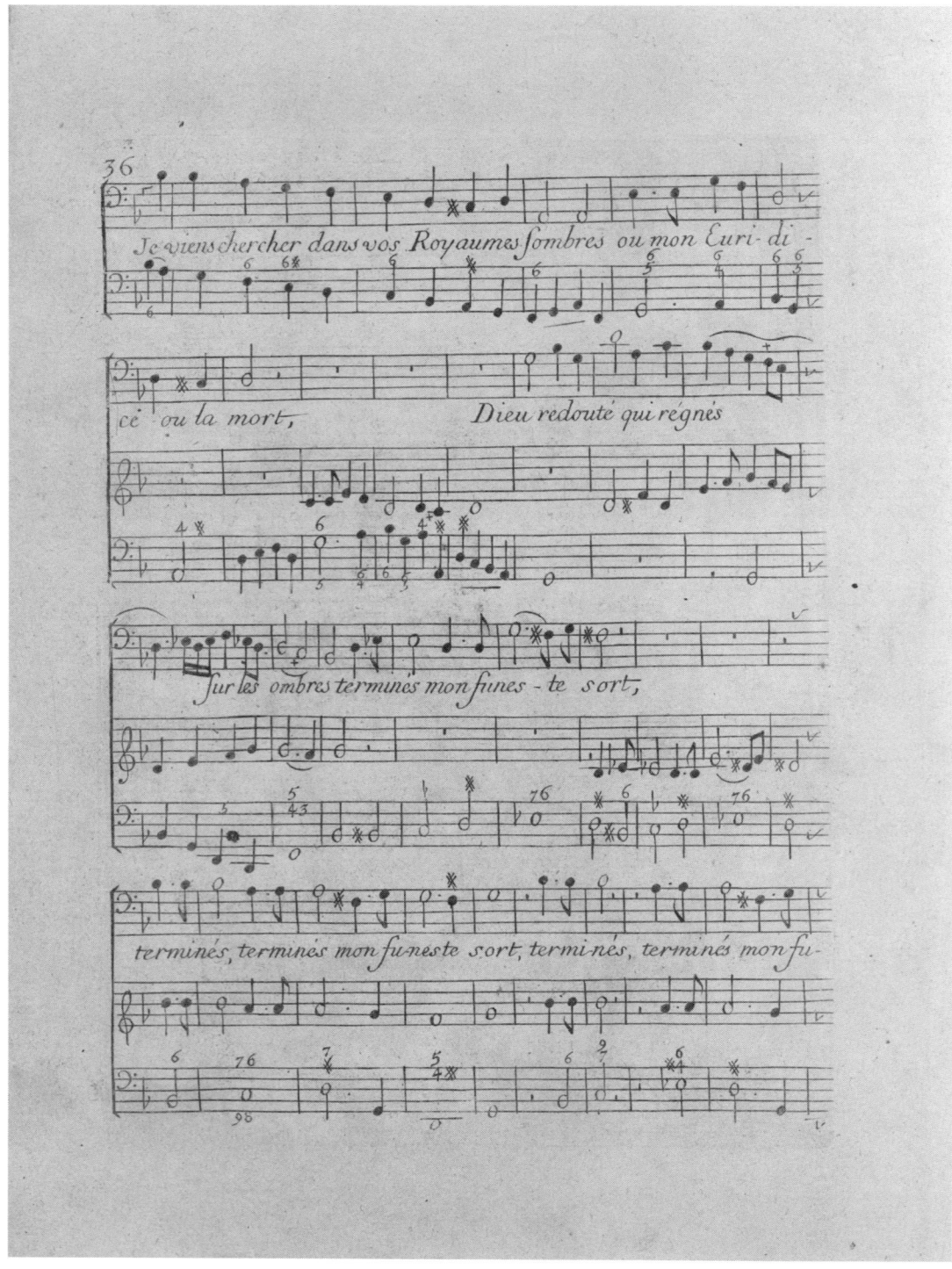

Plate 4. Philippe Courbois, *Cantates françoises à I et II voix sans simphonie et avec simphonie* (Paris: Henri Foucault, 1710), page 36, *Orphée*, "Dieu redouté" (movement 2). Bibliothèque nationale de France, D-8466 (2). Courtesy of the Bibliothèque nationale de France.

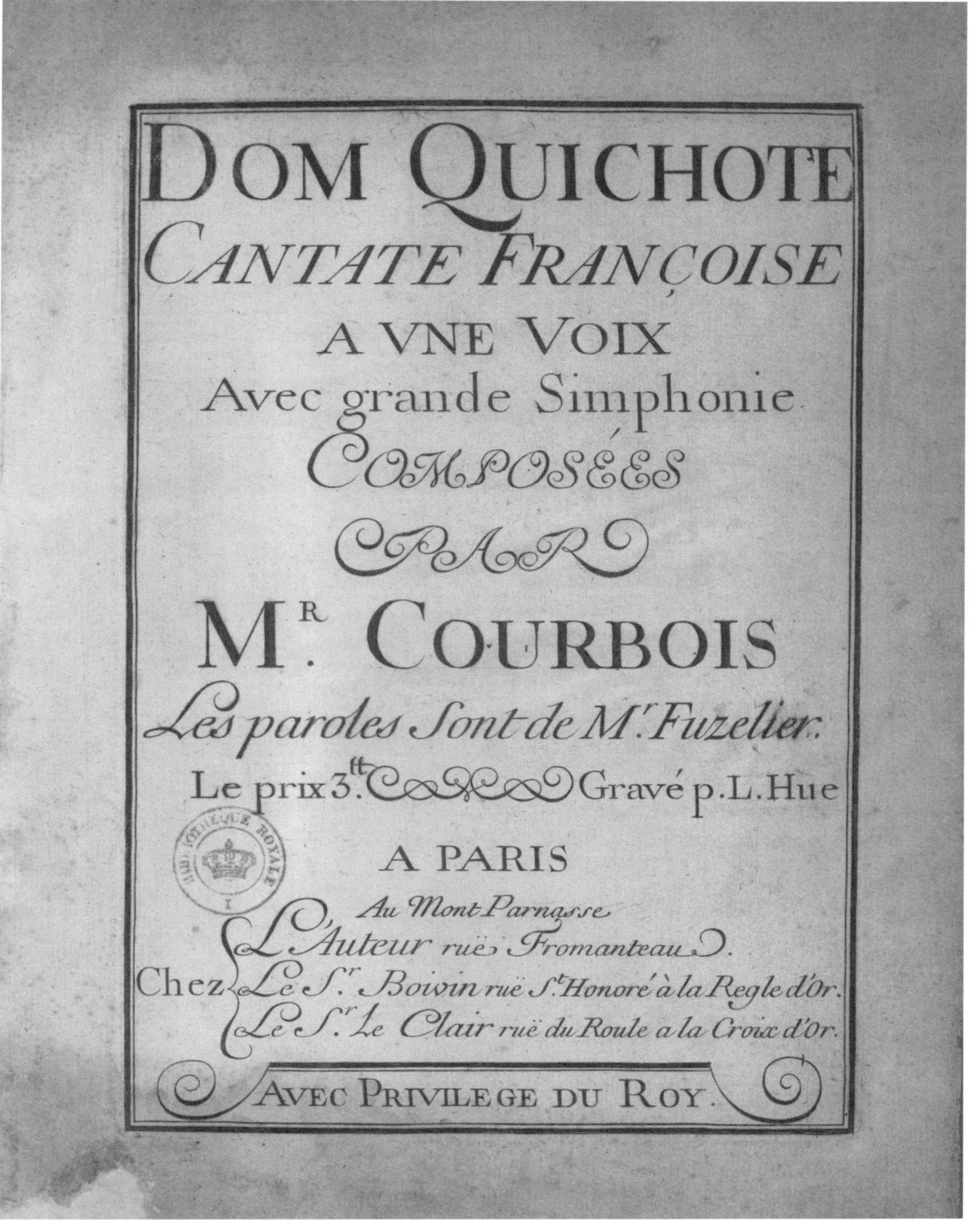

Plate 5. Philippe Courbois, *Dom Quichote, cantate françoise à une voix avec grande simphonie* (Paris: François Boivin, n.d.), title page. Bibliothèque nationale de France, Vm7-163. Courtesy of the Bibliothèque nationale de France.

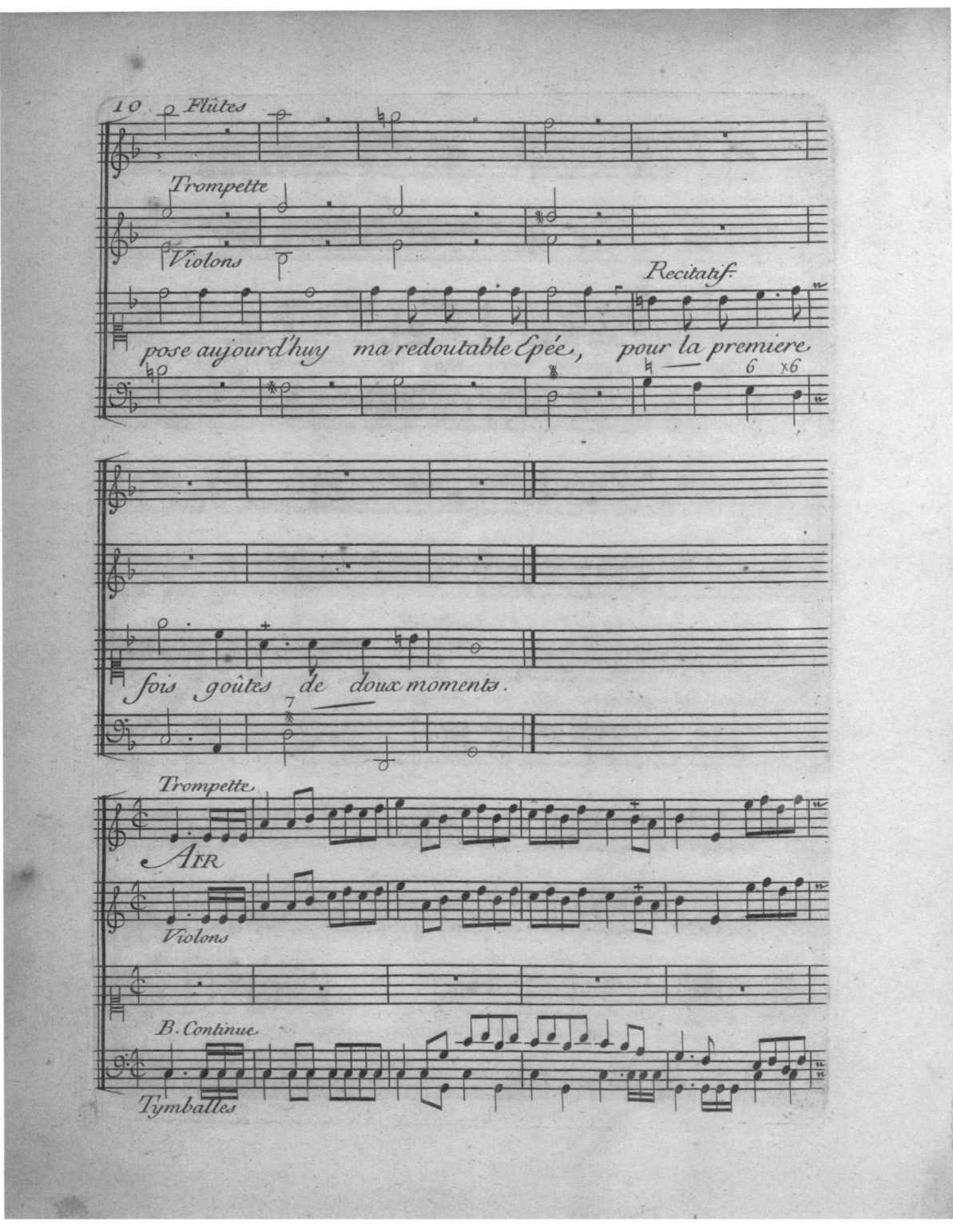

Plate 6. Philippe Courbois, *Dom Quichote, cantate françoise à une voix avec grande simphonie* (Paris: François Boivin, n.d.), page 10, opening of "Vous, qui travaillez" (movement 5). Bibliothèque nationale de France, Vm7-163. Courtesy of the Bibliothèque nationale de France.

Cantates françoises
à I et II voix

Dedication

A son Altesse Serenissime | Madame la Duchesse du Maine

Madame[,]

J'ose vous presenter les premiers essais de mon génie heureux[,] s'ils peuvent amuser un seul moment, V*A*S[.] Je scay[,] Madame[,] que rien n'égale la delicatesse de vôtre gout et la iustesse de vôtre discernement et je me condanne moi même pour cet aveu. Le zelle seul autorise la liberté que je prends d'offrir à V*A*S un tribut si peu digne d'elle et le zelle justifie les moindres hommages[;] excusés le[,] Madame, et souffrés qu'il m'enhardisse à me dire avec un respect profond

De V*A*S | Le tres humble et tres obeïssant serviteur COURBOIS.

To her most serene highness the Duchess of Maine

Madame,

I dare present you the first essays of my fortunate genius so that they may amuse Your Serene Highness, if only for a moment. I know, Madame, that nothing equals the delicacy of your taste and the appropriateness of your discernment, and I condemn myself for this admission. Zeal alone allows the liberty I take to offer Your Serene Highness a tribute so little worthy of you, and zeal justifies the slightest homage; forgive it, Madame, and tolerate that it emboldens me to call myself, with profound respect,

Your Serene Highness's most humble and most obedient servant Courbois.

No. 1. Apollon et Daphné

1. Récitatif

Es- cla- ve nou- veau de l'A- mour, A- pol- lon sou- pi- rait sur les bords du Pé- né- e. Daph- né, s'é- cri- ait- il, hé- las! dans quel sé- jour Ver- rai- je en vous cher- chant, ma pei- ne ter- mi- né- e? Vain- queur d'un mon- stre fu- ri- eux, J'in- sul- tais à l'A- mour et j'ou- tra- geais sa gloi- re; Non! sans les traits char- mants que lui prê- tent vos yeux, Il n'eût ja- mais sur moi rem- por- té la vic- toi- re. Et toi, qui me pu- nis de t'a- voir ou- tra- gé,

En me donnant tes fers tu te tra- his toi- mê- me, Fils de Vé- nus, non, puis- que j'ai- me, Non, non, tu n'es pas bien ven- gé.

2. Air

Lentement

U- ne beau- té ri- gou- reu- se Com- bat en vain nos dé- sirs,

U- ne beau- té ri- gou- reu- se__ Com- bat__ en__ vain__ nos dé-sirs. La__ flam- me__ la__ moins heu- reu- se Don- ne__ tou- jours des plai-sirs, La__ flam- me__ la__ moins heu- reu- se Don- ne__ tou- jour des plai- sirs, La__ flam- me__ la__ moins heu--reu- se Don- ne__ tou- jours__ des plai- sirs.

Fin

Un a--mant, dans sa constance, É-prouve un charme secret,

Un amant, dans sa constance, É-prouve un charme secret, Et l'espoir le récompense Des maux que l'amour lui fait, Et l'espoir le récom-

-pense Des maux que l'amour lui fait, Et l'es-poir le récompense Des maux que l'amour lui fait.

Comme ci-dessus 𝄋
jusqu'à la fin

3. Récitatif

Apollon par ces mots sous un paisible ombrage S'efforçait de calmer ses rigoureux tourments; L'Amour l'avait conduit dans le même bocage Où Daphné se cachait à ses empressements. La nymphe s'y croyait ignorée et tranquille, Mais dans tout l'univers est-il un seul a-

-si- le Con- tre l'a- mour et les a- mants? En- fin, dit A- pol- lon, cher ob- jet que j'a-

-do- re, En- fin je vous re- vois; me fui- rez- vous en- co- re?

[enchaîner]

4. Air

Lentement

[Dessus]

Basse continue

Ah! per- met- tez du moins, en ne m'é- vi- tant pas, Que mon

cœur un moment doute de votre haine,

Ah! permettez du moins, en ne m'évitant pas, Que mon cœur un moment doute de votre haine. Est-il

Fin

temps de me fuir, quand vos divins ap-pas M'ac-ca-blent pour ja-mais d'u-ne cru-el-le chaî-ne, Est-il temps de me fuir, quand vos di-vins ap-pas M'ac-ca-blent pour ja-mais d'u-ne cru-el-le chaî- - ne?

Comme ci-dessus 𝄋
jusqu'à la fin

5. Récitatif

Mais en vain Apollon, amant infortuné, Soupire et court sur les pas de Daphné ; La nymphe, de ses feux craignant la violence, Vole aux rives du fleuve auteur de sa naissance. Ô toi ! s'écria-t-elle, entends ma faible voix, Je t'implore aujourd'hui pour la première fois, Sage Pénée, hélas ! protège l'innocence. C'en est fait, il prend sa défense, Il la change en lau-

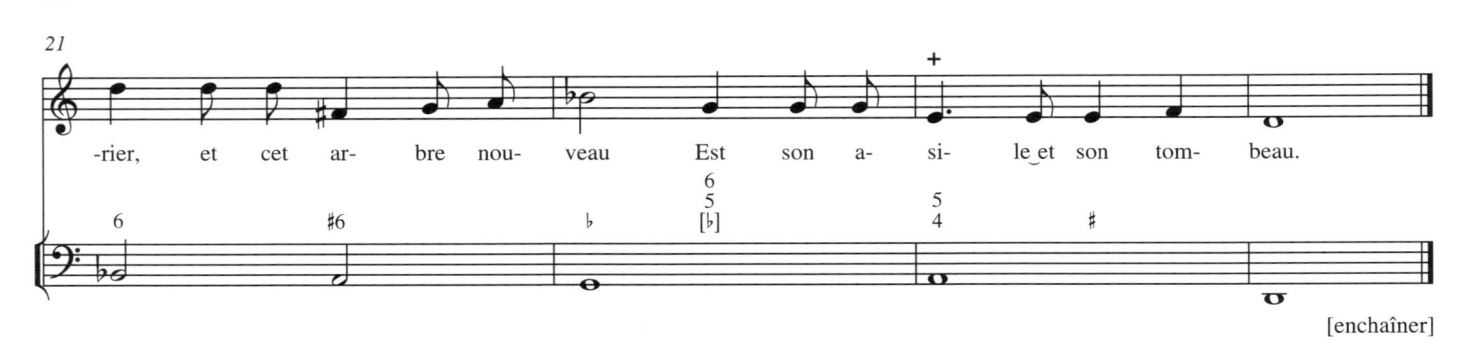

6. [Mesuré]

Lentement

-rier, et cet ar- bre nou- veau Est son a- si- le et son tom- beau.

[enchaîner]

Mal- heu- reux A- pol- lon, tes ta- lents_ et tes char- mes Con- tre un su- per- be cœur sont d'i- nu- ti- les ar- mes; L'A- mour pour te pu- nir l'a- vait ex- près_ for- mé, De ses traits dan- ge- -reux son- geons à nous dé- fen- dre. Ton sort fa- tal doit nous ap- pren- dre Que l'on peut ê- tre ai- ma- ble et n'ê-

7. Air

Lyrics (measures 26-33):
-tre point ai-mé, Ton sort fa-tal doit nous ap--pren-dre Que l'on peut ê-tre ai-ma-ble et n'ê-tre point ai-mé.

Lyrics (Air):
L'art de char-mer est un mys-tè-re Qui ja-mais aux yeux ne pa-raît, L'art de char-mer est un mys-tè-re Qui ja-mais aux yeux ne pa-raît; On ne sait pas lor-squ'on doit

plai- re, On voit seu- le- ment quand on plaît, On ne sait pas lor- squ'on doit

plai- re, On voit seu- le- ment quand on plaît, On ne sait pas lor- squ'on doit

plai- re, On voit seu- le- ment quand on plaît.

Fin

C'est en vain qu'un ob- jet res-

-sem- ble Et la ten- dres- se et la beau- té,

C'est en vain qu'un ob- jet res- sem- ble Et la ten- dres- se et la beau-

15

-té; Sou- vent on les u- nit en- sem- ble Sans en ê- tre mieux é- cou-

-té, Sou- vent on les u- nit en- sem- ble Sans en ê- tre mieux é- cou-

-té, Sou- vent on les u- nit en- sem- ble Sans en ê- tre mieux é- cou- té.

Comme ci-dessus 𝄋
jusqu'à la fin

No. 2. Zéphire et Flore

1. [Récitatif]

Sur les bords d'un ruisseau, Flore dans son empire Attendait l'aimable Zéphire, Quand un nuage sombre et d'affreux sifflements Annoncèrent Borée à la jeune déesse; Aussitôt elle fuit sa jalouse tendresse Et trompe ses empressements. Ah! c'en est fait, dit-il, impitoyable

Mesuré

Flore, Zéphire vous enchante; en vain je vous adore.

[Récitatif]

Vous qui suivez mes lois venez venger mon cœur, Aquilons, punis-

*See "Notes on Performance" in the introduction.

2. Air

18

Que tout ressente ma vengeance,

Puisque tout trahit mon amour.

Ravagez les monts et les plaines,

Fin

Dispersez-vous, tyrans des airs,

Que ne puis-je briser mes chaînes Ainsi que vous rompez vos fers,

Que ne puis-je briser mes chaînes Ain-

-si que vous rom- pez vos fers, Que ne puis- je bri- ser mes chaî- nes Ain- si que vous rom- pez vos fers.

Comme ci-dessus 𝄋
jusqu'à la fin

3. Récitatif

[Dessus] Il dit; aus- si- tôt il ra- va- ge les bois, les co- teaux, les val- lons. Pour cher- cher en tous lieux le ri- val qui l'ou- tra- ge Il vo- le im- pa- ti- ent sur un é- pais nu- a- ge; Il a- mè- ne a- vec lui les fou- gueux A- qui- lons. À pei- ne il dis- pa- raît qu'A- mour ra- mè- ne Flo- re; Les plai- sirs et les

Lentement

jeux ac-com-pa-gnent ses pas. El- le ré- pand par- tout mil- le bril- lants ap-
-pas Que les siens ef- fa- cent en- co- re. Zé- phi- re en- fin se jet- te à ses ge-
-noux; Que vous m'a- lar- mez, lui dit- el- le, Ah! vo- la- ge, d'où ve- nez
vous? Est- ce l'A- mour qui vous rap- pel- le?

[enchaîner]

4. Air

Fort lentement

[Dessus]

[Basse continue]

Vo- tre ri- val, in- grat a-

-mant, Cher- che plus que vous ma pré- sen- ce; Hé- las, hé- las! je crains à tout mo- ment Son ar- deur et vo- -tre in- con- stan- ce, Hé- las, hé- las! je crains à tout mo- ment Son ar- deur et vo- -tre in- con- stan- ce.

Fin

Non, l'a-

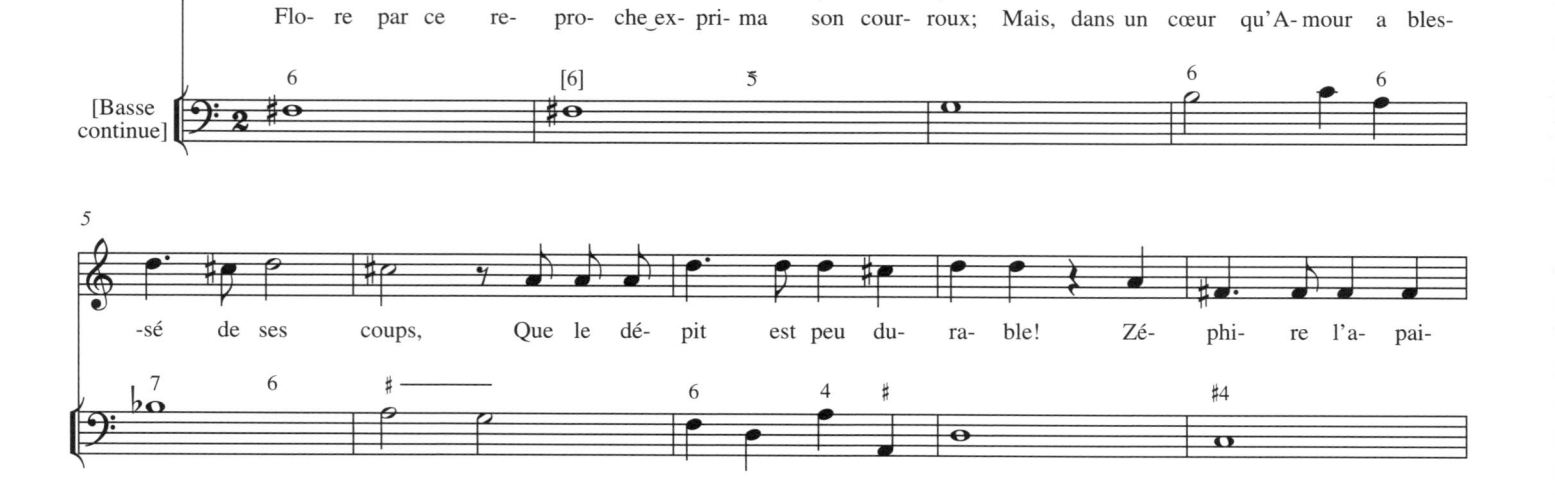

-mour ne ré- pond ja- mais Aux vœux de ma ten- dres- se ex- trê- me; Quand je vois trop ce que je hais, Faut- il voir si peu ce que j'ai- me, Quand je vois trop ce que je hais, Faut- il voir si peu ce que j'ai- me?

Comme ci-dessus 𝄋
jusqu'à la fin

5. Récitatif

[Dessus] Flo- re par ce re- pro- che ex- pri- ma son cour- roux; Mais, dans un cœur qu'A- mour a bles- sé de ses coups, Que le dé- pit est peu du- ra- ble! Zé- phi- re l'a- pai-

6. Air

-sa par ses soins les plus doux; Un amant qui sait plaire est rarement coupable. Tandis que déchiré par mille vains désirs, Borée à la fureur abandonne son âme; L'heureux Zéphire et l'objet de sa flamme Se font de ses tourments mille nouveaux plaisirs.

Tendrement

Tendre Amour, dans ton empire Un cœur jaloux qui soupire N'éprouve qu'un sort fatal, Tendre A-

-mour, dans ton em- pi- re Un cœur ja- loux qui sou- pi- re N'é-prou- ve qu'un sort fa- tal. Par ses soins et ses a- lar- mes Il a- jou- te en- core des char- mes Au bon- heur de son ri- val, Par ses soins et ses a- lar- mes Il a- jou- te en- core des char- mes Au bon- heur de son ri- val.

Fin

C'est en vain qu'il per- sé- vè- re,

C'est en vain qu'il per- sé- vè- re: Plus il s'ef- for- ce de plai- re Et moins il se fait ai- mer; Tan- dis que près de sa bel- le C'est l'a- mant le moins fi- dè- le Qui la sait mieux en- flam- mer, Tan- dis que près de sa bel- le C'est l'a- mant le moins fi- dè- le Qui la sait mieux en- flam- mer.

Comme ci-dessus 𝄋
jusqu'à la fin

No. 3. L'Amant timide

1. Récitatif

[Haute-contre]
[Basse continue]

La beau-té qu'a-do-re Phi-lè-ne A-vait de son bon-heur fix-é le cher mo-ment; Le ber-ger, ré-veil-lé par cet es-poir char-mant, N'at-tend pas que le jour, qui doit fi-nir sa pei-ne, An-non-ce à l'ar-deur qui l'en-traî-ne Les plus doux plai-sirs d'un a-mant. Il sort im-pa-ti-ent de sa re-trai-te ob-scu-re, L'A-mour l'é-clai-re, en vain la nuit cou-vre ses yeux, Et par ces mots pres-sants ce ber-ger la con-ju-re De cé-der au so-leil la car-riè-re des cieux.

2. Air

charmante aurore, Venez, brillez, charmante aurore; De l'aimable objet que j'adore Annoncez-moi l'heureux retour.

Comme ci-dessus 𝄋
jusqu'à la fin

3. Récitatif

[Haute-contre] Mais, c'en est fait: nuit, vous disparaissez.

[Basse continue]

Déjà le jour naissant embellit ces bocages, L'Amour y réunit les oiseaux dispersés; Ah! je verrai bientôt sous ces charmants om-

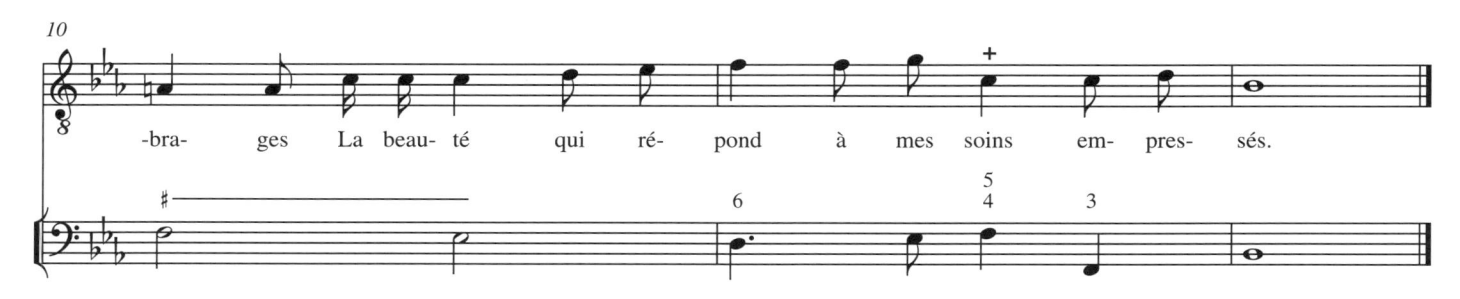

-bra- ges La beau- té qui ré- pond à mes soins em- pres- sés.

4. Air

Gracieusement

[Haute-contre]

[Basse continue]

Vous qui dif- fé- rez la pré- sen- ce De l'ai- ma- ble ob- jet de mes vœux, Ter- mi- nez mon im- pa- ti- en- ce, Vo- lez, vo- lez, mo- ments trop ri- gou- -reux, Vous qui dif- fé- pré- -sen- ce De l'ai- ma- ble ob- jet de mes vœux, Ter- mi- nez mon im- pa- ti- en- ce, Vo- lez, mo- ments trop ri- gou-

-reux, Vo- lez, _____ vo- lez, ___ mo- ments trop ri- gou- reux,

Ter- mi- nez mon im- pa- ti- en- ce, Vo- lez, mo- ments trop ri- gou-

-reux, Ter- mi- nez mon im- pa- ti- en- ce, Vo- lez, mo- ments trop ri- gou- reux.

Fin

Vous qui de- vez m'of- frir Syl- vi- e, Doux mo- ment, com- blez mon es-

-poir, Vous qui de- vez m'of- frir Syl-

-vi- e, Doux mo- ment, com- blez mon es- poir. Que ne puis- je ô- ter de ma vi- e Ceux que je pas- se sans la voir, Que ne puis- je ô- ter de ma vi- e Ceux que je pas- se sans la voir, Que ne puis- je ô- ter de ma vi- e Ceux que je pas- se sans la voir!

Comme ci-dessus 𝄋
jusqu'à la fin

5. Récitatif

[Haute-contre] Tan- dis que le ber- ger dans un bois so- li- tai- re Par de tendres sou--haits a- mu- se sa lan- gueur, L'A- mour a- mè- ne sa ber- gè- re; Phi- lène a- mou- reux, sûr de plai- re, Lui de- man- de aus- si- tôt le prix de son ar- deur. Syl- vie à ces trans-

-ports feint son cour- roux sé- vè- re; Le ber- ger, a- bu- sé par sa faus- se ri- gueur, En la crai- gnant mé- ri- te sa co- lè- re, Et n'o- sant la ra- vir, perd en- fin son bon- heur.

6. Air

[Haute-contre]

[Basse continue]

Dans le mo- ment le plus ten- dre, Un ob- jet prêt à se ren- dre Feint tou- jours de ré- sis- ter; Et, vic- ti- me de la gloi- re, Il dis- pu- te u- ne vic- toi- re Qu'il ne veut pas rem- por- ter.

Fin

A- mants, domptez votre crainte, Et qu'une colère feinte Ne trouble pas vos désirs; Songez, quand l'Amour vous guide, Qu'il égare un cœur timide Dans la route des plaisirs. Songez, -sirs.

Comme ci-dessus 𝄋
jusqu'à la fin

No. 4. Orphée

1. [Récitatif]

Ô Ciel! disait Orphée, ô disgrâce fatale! Vous mourez, Eurydice, hélas, hélas! Attendez, je descends sur la rive infernale; Que ma lyre en ce jour ne m'abandonne pas.

Lentement

Je vois déjà le terrible ri-

-vage Où Mercure confond les bergers et les rois. Caron est attendri: pour la première fois, Il m'offre dans sa barque un facile passage,

37

Et Cerbère attentif, dans son antre sauvage, Du monarque des morts trahit les dures lois. Je vois Pluton; Amour, viens animer ma voix.

2. [Air]

ombres, Terminez mon funeste sort,

Dieu redouté, qui régnez _____ sur les _

ombres, Terminez, terminez mon funeste

sort. Je viens chercher dans vos royaumes sombres Ou mon Eury-

-di- ce ou la mort. Dieu re-dou--té, qui ré- gnez sur les om- bres, Ter- mi--nez mon fu- nes- te sort, Ter- mi- nez, ter- mi- nez mon fu- nes- te sort,

Ter- mi- nez, ter- mi- nez mon fu- nes- te sort.

3. Récitatif

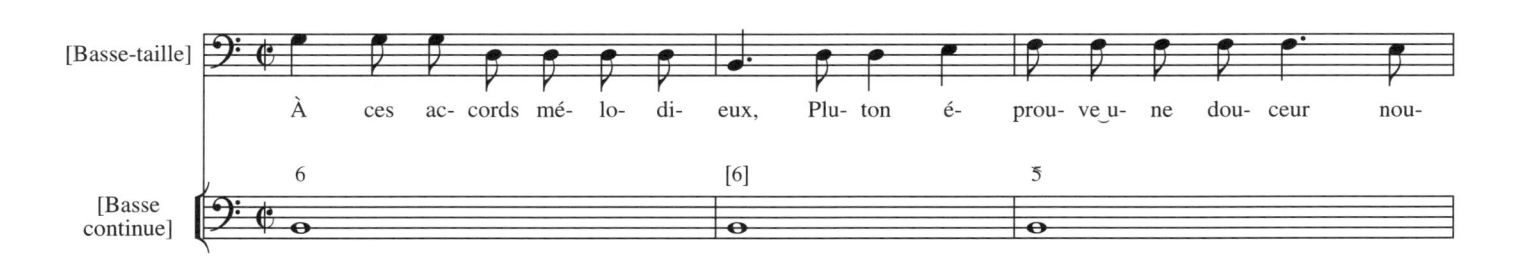

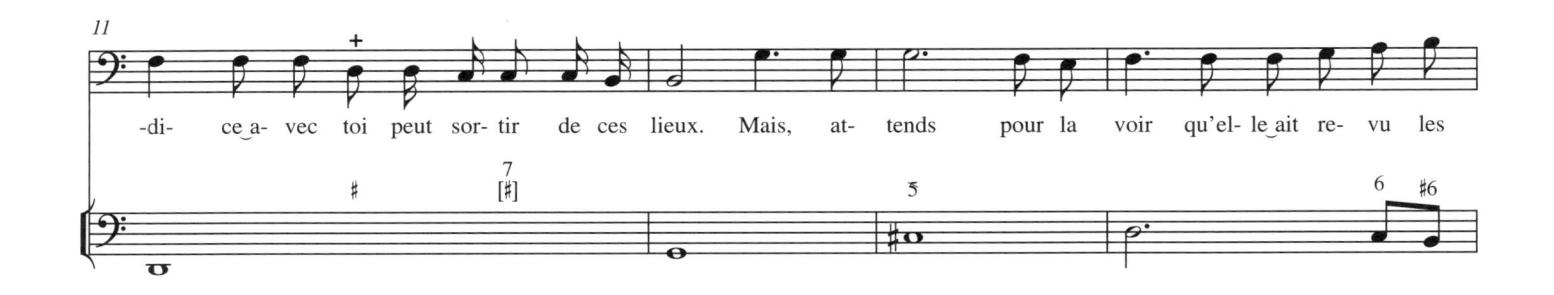

[Basse-taille]: À ces ac- cords mé- lo- di- eux, Plu- ton é- prou- ve u- ne dou- ceur nou- vel- le. Fils d'A- pol- lon, dit- il, que la par- que cru- el- le Cè- de à ton feu vic- to- ri- eux: Il ef- fa- ce l'hor- reur de la nuit é- ter- nel- le, Eu- ry- di- ce a- vec toi peut sor- tir de ces lieux. Mais, at- tends pour la voir qu'el- le ait re- vu les cieux: C'est la loi que j'im- po- se à ton a- mour fi- dè- le. Un seul de tes re-

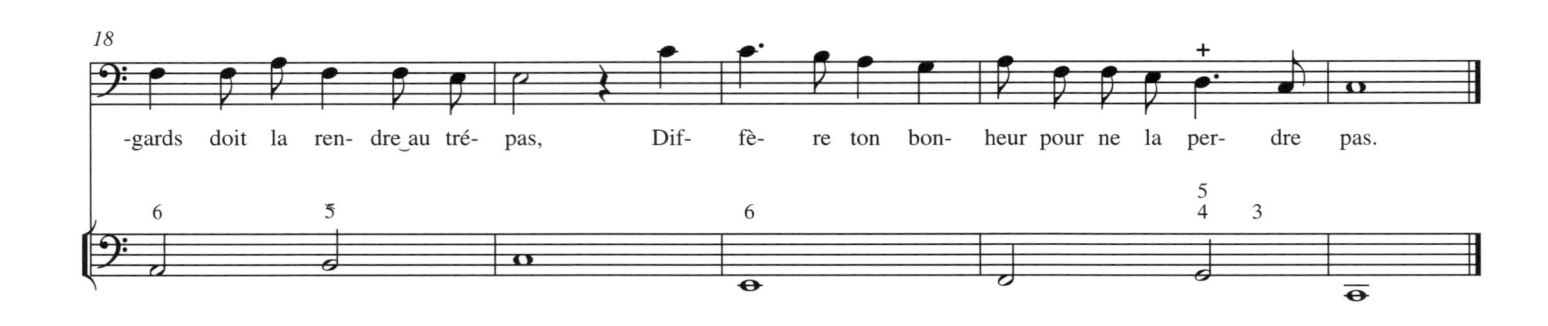

-gards doit la ren- dre au tré- pas, Dif- fè- re ton bon- heur pour ne la per- dre pas.

4. Air

Gai

Trompette

[Basse-taille]

[Basse continue]

Tpt.

BT

Peut- on re- fu-

B.c.

43

-re Jus- qu'au fond du som- bre sé- jour, Il por- te ses feux et sa gloi- - - re Jus- qu'au fond, jus- qu'au fond du som- bre sé- jour. Peut- on re- fu- ser la vic- toi- - re, Peut-

-on re- fu- ser la vic- toi- - re Aux doux ef- forts du ten- dre A-

-mour? Il por- te ses feux et sa gloi- - -

-re Jus- qu'au fond du som- bre sé- jour,

Il por- te ses feux et sa gloi- -

- re Jus- qu'au fond, jus- qu'au fond du som- bre sé- jour, Jus- qu'au fond du som- bre sé- jour.

Fin

On y res- pec- te en- core ses ar- mes,

On y res- pec- te en- core ses ar- mes, Les ombres pous- sent des sou- pirs, Et le sou- ve- nir de ses char- mes

5. Récitatif

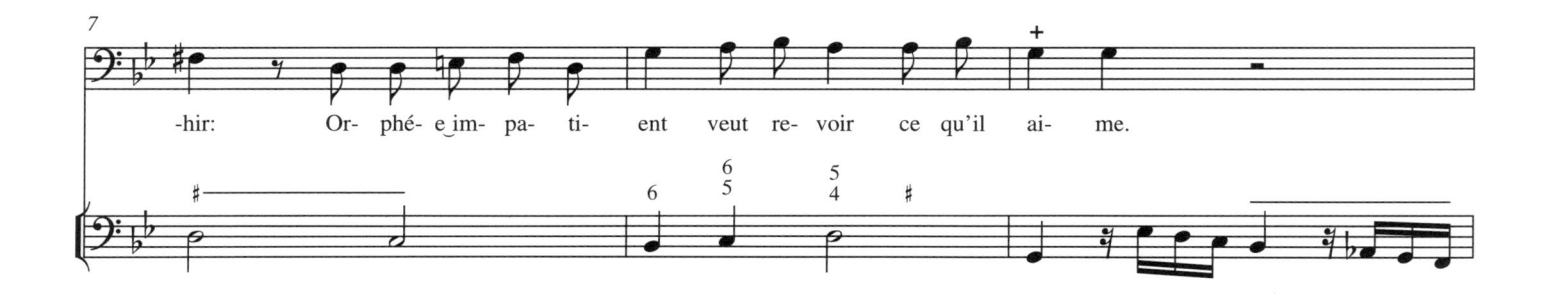

Déjà loin des forêts du paisible Élysée, Eurydice volait sur les traces d'Orphée; Mais l'Amour imprudent est prêt à se trahir: Orphée impatient veut revoir ce qu'il aime.

Tendre époux, arrêtez, vous vous perdez vous-même: Vous devez plutôt obéir À la loi de Pluton qu'à votre ardeur extrême. C'en est fait, Eurydice échappe à vos souhaits; La parque dans vos yeux contre elle prend des armes. Dieux! en la regardant, vous effacez ses charmes, Et l'enfer à vos yeux se ferme pour jamais.

6. Air

49

doux

doux

Ah! doit-on d'un feu trop tendre É-cou-ter tou-jours l'ar-deur, Ah! doit-on d'un feu trop tendre É-cou-ter tou-jours l'ar-deur? Lor-squ'on ne sait pas l'at-ten-dre, On perd sou-vent son bon-

-heur, Lor- squ'on ne sait pas l'at- ten- dre, On perd sou- vent son bon-

-heur, Lor- squ'on ne sait pas l'at- ten- dre, On perd sou- vent son bon- heur.

Fin

Quel est d'un cœur qui sou- pi- re Le fa- tal é- ga- re- ment,

Quel est d'un cœur qui sou- pi- re Le fa- tal é- ga- re- ment! Il ris- que un bien qu'il dé- si- re Pour l'a- van- cer d'un mo- ment, Il ris- que un bien qu'il dé- si- re Pour l'a- van- cer d'un mo- ment, Il ris- que un bien qu'il dé- si- re Pour l'a- van- cer d'un mo- ment.

Comme ci-dessus 𝄋 jusqu'à la fin

No. 5. Ariane

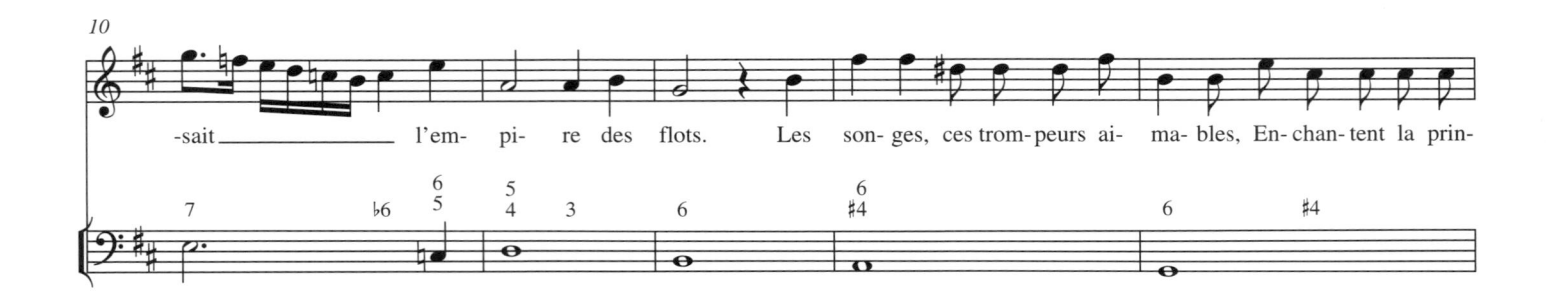

1. Récitatif

Sous les arbres épais d'un paisible bocage Ariane dormait dans l'île de Naxos, Tandis que son amant volage Traversait l'empire des flots. Les songes, ces trompeurs aimables, Enchantent la princesse et par de feints plaisirs Diffèrent des maux véritables; Et dans ces instants favorables L'Amour à la douleur dérobe ses soupirs.

[enchaîner]

2. [Air]

Ne vous réveillez pas encore, Beaux yeux, vous ne verrez que trop tôt vos mal-

-heurs, Ne vous ré-veil-lez pas en- co- re, Beaux
yeux, vous ne ver- rez que trop tôt vos mal- heurs.
Sem- bla- bles à ceux de l'au- ro- re, Vous ne vous ou- vri-
-rez que pour ver- ser des pleurs, que pour ver- ser
des pleurs. Ne vous ré- veil- lez

3. Récitatif

Mais l'Amour interrompt les songes qui l'amusent; Ariane s'é- -veille, ô funeste moment! Son cœur croit que ses yeux l'abusent Et veut justifi-

*See "Notes on Performance" in the introduction.

9
D
-er son in- fi- dè- le a- mant. Tout la dé- trom- pe; en- fin el- le court sur la ri- ve, Et son dés- or- dre ex-
B.c.
13
D
-po- se à la clar- té du jour Des ap- pas ré- ser- vés aux re- gards de l'A- mour. Les ac-
B.c.
17
D
-cents de sa voix plain- ti- ve Font gé- mir a- près eux les é- chos d'a- len- tour; In-
B.c.
22
Fl.
D
-grat, dit- el- le, hé- las! tu fuis et je t'a- do- re. Tu
B.c.
28
D
fuis, quel prix de mes bien- faits! Peux- tu te sou- ve- nir du fa- tal Mi- no- tau- re,
B.c.

32

D: Et tra- hir mes fai- bles at- traits? Que vois- je? le vais-

36

D: -seau du per- fi- de Thé- sé- e; Que ce fu- nes- te ob- jet re- dou- ble mes fu-

39

D: -reurs! Ah! c'en est fait,

42

D: ah! mon- trez, Dieux ven- geurs, Que vous ê- tes l'ap- pui de la foi mé- pri- sé- e.

[enchaîner]

4. [Air]

Prélude
Fort vite

[Violon]

[Dessus]

[Basse continue]

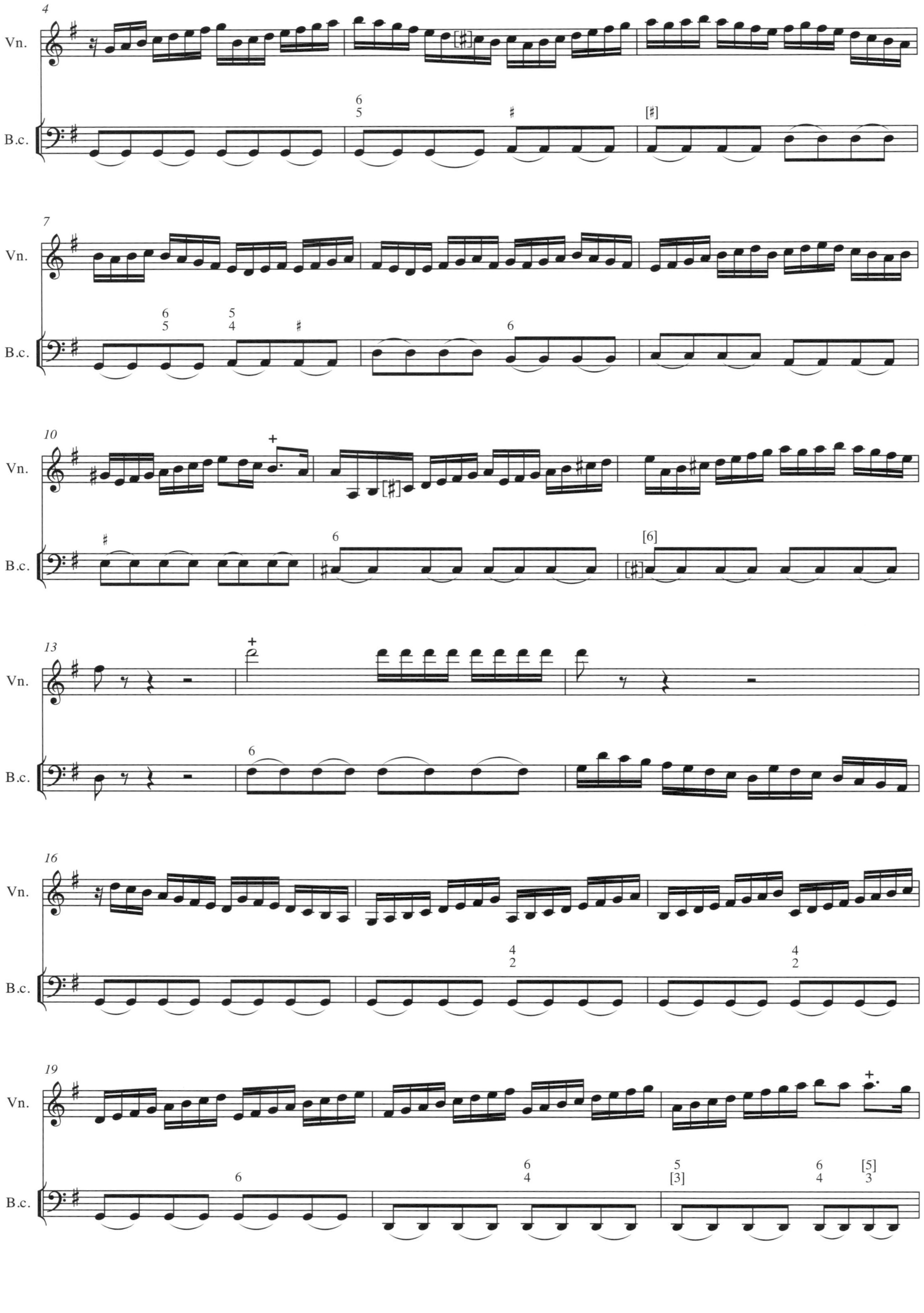
4
Vn.
B.c.
7
Vn.
B.c.
10
Vn.
B.c.
13
Vn.
B.c.
16
Vn.
B.c.
19
Vn.
B.c.

Dieu des mers, ser- vez mon cour- roux, Que le ciel é- cla- -te, qu'il ton- ne; Vents fu- ri- eux, con- ju- rez tous Con- tre un a- mant qui m'a- ban- don- -ne. Frap- pez, frap- pez, du plus mor- tel ef-

-froi, Le cœur d'un in- grat qui m'of- fen- se, Fai- tes qu'il souf- fre au tant que moi; Et vous rem- pli- rez ma ven- gean- ce. Dieu des mers, ser- vez mon cour- roux, Que le ciel é- cla- te, qu'il ton- ne;

Vents fu- ri- eux, con- ju- rez tous Con- tre un a- mant qui m'a- ban- -don- ne.

5. Récitatif

[Dessus] Quel Dieu vient d'A- ri- a- ne a- pai- ser la dou- leur? De l'In- de re- nom- mé[e], c'est le fa- meux vain- queur. L'A- mour lui prê- te- t-il son arc et sa puis- san- ce? Quel

Mesuré

char- me sur- pre- nant, quel- le promp- te in- con- stan- ce!

Récitatif

De la triste princesse il enchante le cœur, Par un brillant hommage, il répare sa gloire Et venge les affronts que ses yeux ont reçus; Du perfide Thésée elle perd la mémoire, Et tout son cœur se livre à l'amour de Bacchus.

6. Air

Tendrement

Beau- tés dont on tra- hit les char- mes, Et qu'un vo- la- ge o- se ou- tra- -ger, Ne li- vrez pas vos yeux aux lar- mes; Qu'ils vous prê- tent plu- tôt des ar- mes Pour le pu- nir__ et vous ven- ger,

Beau- tés dont on__ tra- hit__ les char- mes, Et qu'un vo- la- ge o- se ou- tra-

-ger, Ne li- vrez pas vos yeux__ aux lar- mes; Qu'ils vous prê- tent plu- tôt des

ar- mes Pour le pu- nir et vous ven- ger, Qu'ils vous prê- tent plu- tôt des ar- mes Pour le pu- nir et vous ven- ger.

Fin

Pour u- ne vic- toi- re nou-

-vel- le Pré- pa- rez vos ai- ma- bles traits, Pour u-

-ne victoire nouvelle Préparez vos aimables traits; Et qu'une conquête plus belle De la perte d'un infidèle Dédommage vos doux attraits, Et qu'une conquête plus belle De la perte d'un infidèle Dédommage vos doux attraits. Beautés dont on trahit les

Comme ci-dessus 𝄋
jusqu'à la fin

No. 6. Jason et Médée

1. [Récitatif]

Que vois-je? c'est Médée: elle vient dans ces lieux. Hélas! que je crains qu'à ses yeux L'amour qui la trahit ne s'accuse lui-même. Que deviendrais-je? ô ciel! si ma trop vive ardeur Lui décelait l'objet que j'aime; Feignons pour tromper sa fureur.

2. [Duo]

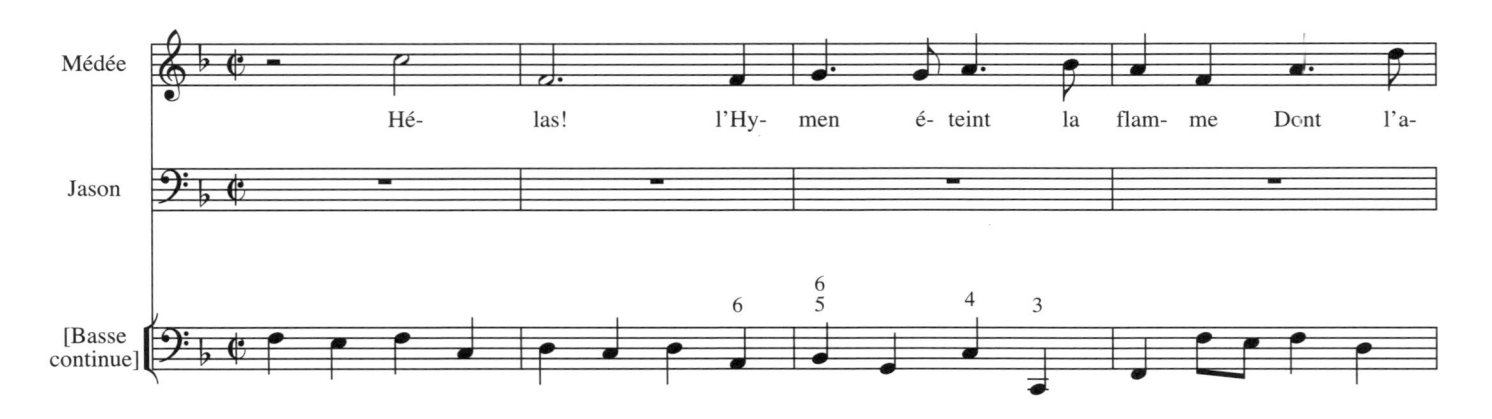

Médée: Hélas! l'Hymen éteint la flamme Dont l'a-

-mour brû- lait vo- tre cœur; Je ne rè- gne plus sur vo- tre âme, Vos

Hé-

yeux m'ap-pren- nent mon mal- heur,

-las! l'Hy- men é- teint la flam- me Dont l'a- mour brû- lait

Hé-

vo- tre cœur; Je ne rè- gne plus sur vo- tre âme, Vos

-las! l'Hy- men é- teint la flam- me Dont l'a- mour brû- lait vo- tre cœur, Hé-

yeux m'ap-pren- nent mon mal- heur, Hé- las! l'Hy- men é- teint la flam- me Dont l'a-

-las! l'Hy- men é- teint la flam- me Dont l'a- mour brû- lait vo- tre

-mour brû- lait vo- tre cœur; Je ne rè- gne plus sur vo-

cœur; Je ne rè- gne plus sur votre âme, Hé- las! l'Hy-

-tre âme, Vos yeux m'ap- pren- nent mon mal- heur,

-men é- teint la flam- me Dont l'a- mour brû- lait vo- tre cœur;

Hé- las! l'Hy- men é- teint la flam- me Dont l'a-

Je ne rè- gne plus sur votre âme, Vos yeux m'ap- prennent

-mour brû- lait vo- tre cœur; Je ne

mon malheur, Hélas! l'Hymen éteint la flamme Dont l'amour brûlait votre cœur, Hélas! l'Hymen éteint la flamme, Dont l'amour brûlait votre cœur; Je ne règne plus sur votre âme, Vos yeux m'apprennent mon malheur.

(basse) règne plus sur votre âme, Vos yeux m'apprennent mon malheur, Hélas! l'Hymen éteint la flamme, Je ne règne plus sur votre âme, Je ne règne plus sur votre âme, Vos yeux m'apprennent mon malheur.

3. Récitatif

MÉDÉE

Ciel! quand d'un feu nouveau son âme est possédée, Quand Créuse a su l'engager, Jason m'accuse de changer. Ingrat, songes-tu bien que tu trahis Médée? Ne te souvient-il plus du pouvoir dangereux Qui du séjour des morts m'ouvre les noirs abîmes? Perfide, en oubliant mon amour malheureux, As-tu donc oublié ses crimes? N'ont-ils pas à tes yeux assez fait éclater Et ma tendresse et ma puissance? Il n'en est pas un seul qui ne dût ex- ci- ter Ta crain- te et ta re- con- nais- san- ce.

[enchaîner]

4. Air

Fort vite

Médée

[Basse continue]

Tri- om- phez, ven- gean- ce, Ve- nez m'ir- ri- ter; Souf- frir u- ne of- fen- se C'est la mé- ri-

-ter, Tri- om- phez, ven- gean- ce, Ve- nez m'ir- ri-

-ter; Souf- frir u- ne of- fen- se C'est la mé- ri- ter.

Que l'a- mour mur- mu- re, Sui- vons la fu- reur; Per- dons le par- ju- re Dont je perds le

Fin

cœur, Que l'a- mour mur- mu- re, Sui- vons la fu- reur; Per- dons le par- ju- re Dont je perds le cœur.

Tri- om- phez, ven-

Comme ci-dessus 𝄋
jusqu'à la fin

5. Récitatif

JASON

Hé- las! gar- dez- vous bien de croi- re Ce que votre fu- reur vous in- spi- re au- jour- d'hui. La prin- ces- se dé- fend vos jours et vo- tre gloi- re, Mon res- pect et mes soins vous don- nent son ap- pui, Cré- on est pré- ve- nu, contre vous on l'a- ni- me; Vous pour- riez ê- tre sa vic- ti- me Sans le se- cours d'un cœur plus gé- né- reux que lui.

[Basse continue]

[enflé]*

*See "Notes on Performance" in the introduction.

6. Air

pas Qu'on ra- vis- se un cœur à vos char- mes Où vous bril- lez; ne crai- gnez

pas Qu'on ra- vis- se un cœur à vos char- mes Où vous bril- lez; ne crai- gnez

pas Qu'on ra- vis- se un cœur à vos char- mes.
Fin

On res- sent en vain d'au- tres

feux, Dès qu'on vous voit, on est vo- la- ge, Mais ja- mais on ne se dé-

-ga- ge Quand on sou- pi- re dans vos nœuds,

27 On res- sent en vain d'au- tres feux, Dès qu'on vous voit, on est vo- la- ge, Mais ja- mais on ne se dé- -ga- ge Quand on sou- pi- re dans vos nœuds, Mais ja- mais on ne se dé- -ga- ge Quand on sou- pi- re dans vos nœuds.

Comme ci-dessus 𝄋
jusqu'à la fin

7. Récitatif

MÉDÉE
Ja- son, tu veux ca- cher ta flam- me et ton ef- froi Pour é- vi- ter ma ven- gean- ce fa- -ta- le; Ah! tu trem- bles pour ma ri- va- le Quand tu feins de trem- bler pour

[Basse continue]

JASON
moi. Non, Créuse à vos lois ne me rend pas rebelle: Mon cœur par ses beaux yeux n'a pas été surpris. De tous les soins que j'ai pour elle, C'est vous, hélas! qui me devez le prix.

MÉDÉE
Ah! contre vos soupirs je ne puis me défendre; Si vous trompez mon cœur trop tendre, Gardez-vous de le détromper.

JASON
À vos transports jaloux gardez-vous de vous rendre; Votre cœur, s'il m'aimait, devrait les dissiper.

[enchaîner]

8. [Duo]

Médée: Calmez mes soupçons et mes peines, Régnez,

6
— tri- om- phez, ten- dre A- mour,
Cal- mez ses soup- çons et ses pei- nes, Ré-
12
-gnez, tri- om- phez, ten- dre A- mour, tri- om- phez,
17
Cal- mez mes soup- çons et mes pei- nes, Ré- gnez,
tri- om- phez, ten- dre A- mour, Cal- mez ses soup-
22
ré- gnez, tri- om- phez,
-çons et ses pei- nes, Ré- gnez, tri- om- phez,

27
tri- om- phez, ten- dre A- mour.
tri- om- phez, ten- dre A- mour. Il faut que l'Hy- men en ce jour Vous ait pour ga-
32
Il faut que l'Hy- men en ce jour Vous ait pour ga- rant de ses chaî-
-rant de ses chaî- nes, Il faut que l'Hy- men en ce
37
-nes. Cal- mez mes soup- çons et mes pei- nes, Ré- gnez,
jour Vous ait pour ga- rant de ses chaî- nes. Cal- mez ses soup- çons et ses
43
Cal- mez mes soup- çons et mes pei- nes, Ré- gnez,
pei- nes, Ré- gnez, ré- gnez, tri- om-

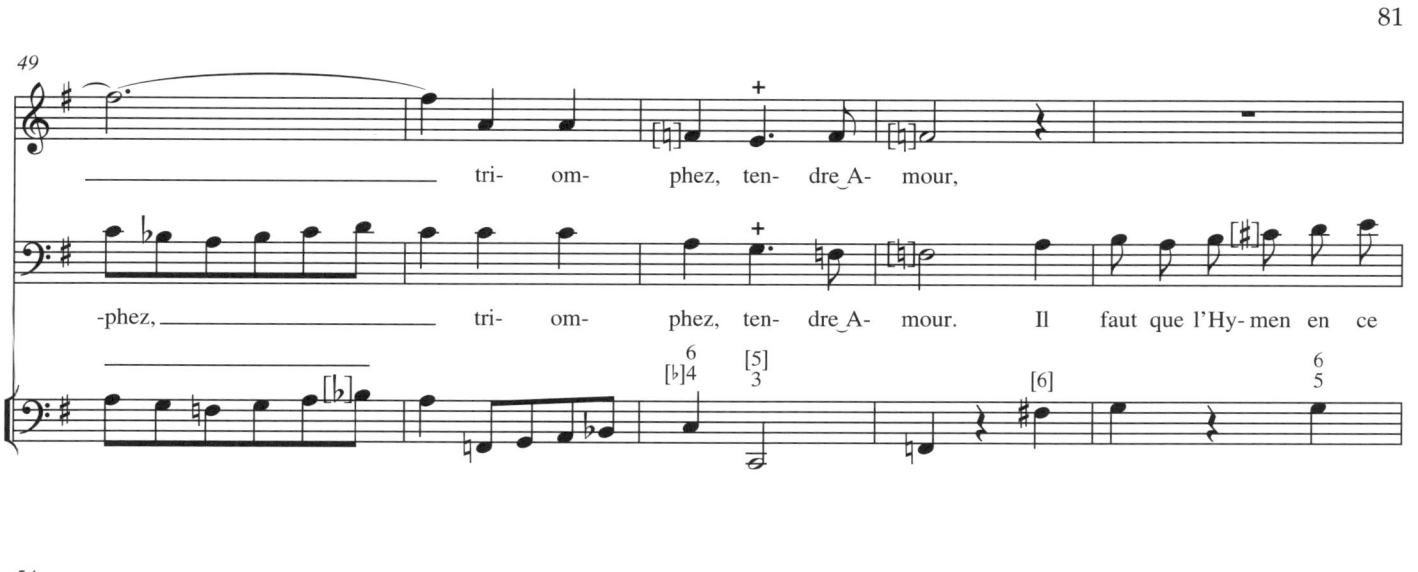

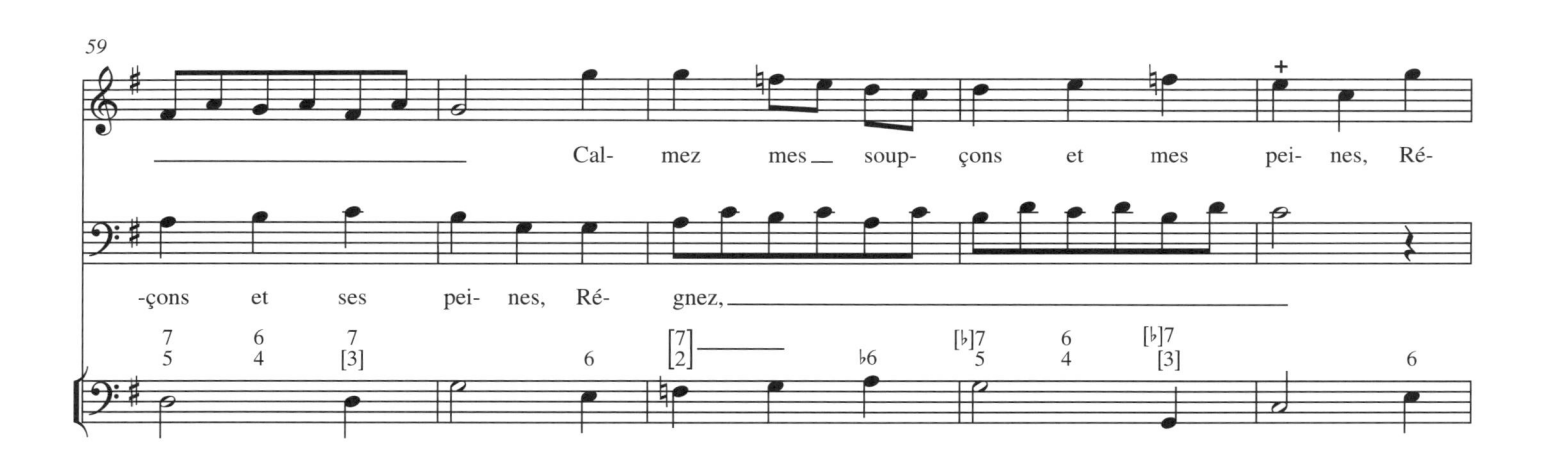

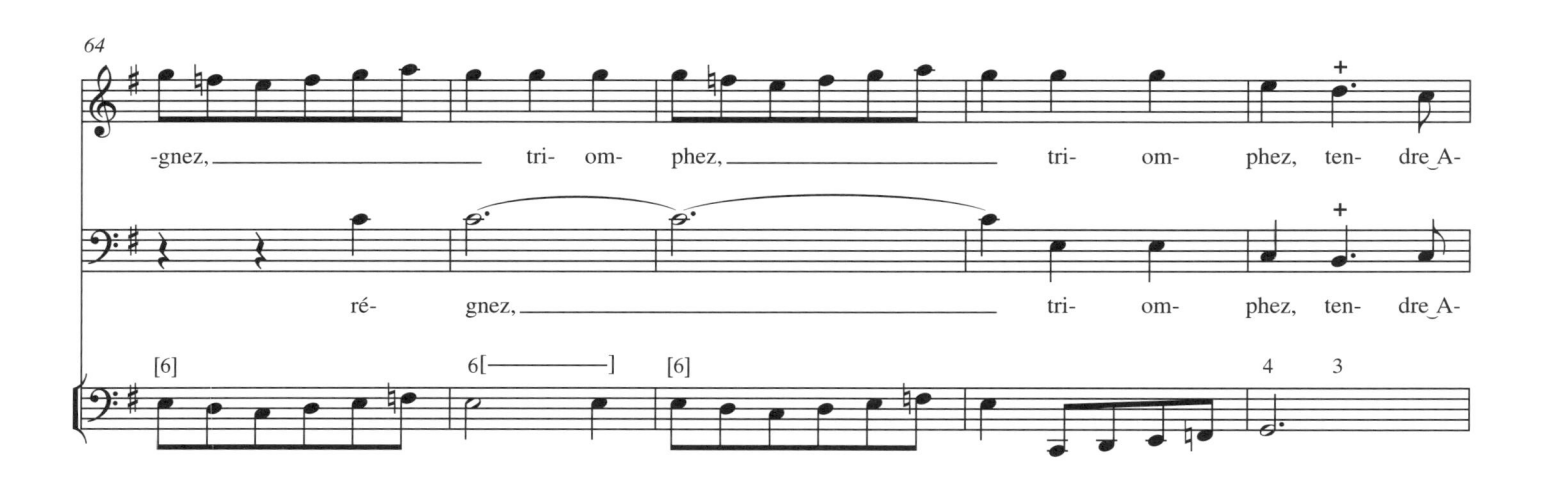

tri- om- phez, ten- dre Amour,

-phez, tri- om- phez, ten- dre Amour. Il faut que l'Hy- men en ce

Cal- mez mes soup- çons et mes pei- nes, Ré- gnez,

jour Vous ait pour ga- rant de ses chaî- nes, Cal- mez ses soup-

Cal- mez mes soup- çons et mes pei- nes, Ré-

-çons et ses pei- nes, Ré- gnez,

-gnez, tri- om- phez, tri- om- phez, ten- dre A-

ré- gnez, tri- om- phez, ten- dre A-

69
-mour. Il faut que l'Hy- men en ce
-mour. Il faut que l'Hy- men en ce jour Vous ait pour ga- rant de ses chaî-
74
jour Vous ait pour ga- rant de ses chaî- nes. Cal- mez mes soup-
-nes. Cal- mez ses soup- çons et ses pei- nes, Ré- gnez,
79
-çons et mes pei- nes, Ré- gnez, tri- om- phez, tri- om-
ré- gnez, tri- om- phez, tri- om-
85
-phez, ten- dre A- mour. Il faut que l'Hy- men en ce jour Vous ait pour ga- rant de ses
-phez, ten- dre A- mour. Il faut que l'Hy- men en ce jour Vous ait pour ga- rant de ses

chaî- - - nes. Cal- mez mes soup-
chaî- - - nes.

-çons et mes pei- nes, Ré- gnez, Cal-
Cal- mez ses soup- çons et ses pei- nes, Ré-

-mez mes soup- çons et mes pei- nes, Ré- gnez, tri- om-
-gnez, ré- gnez, tri- om-

-phez, ten- dre Amour, Ré- gnez, tri- om- phez,
-phez, ten- dre Amour, Ré- gnez, tri- om- phez,

triom- phez, tendre Amour, Régnez, triom-

triom- phez, tendre Amour, Régnez, triom-

-phez, tendre A- mour.

-phez, tendre A- mour.

No. 7. Dom Quichote

1. Prélude

86

Gai

2. Récitatif

[Taille]
Dom Qui-cho-te, en-fon-cé dans la mon-ta-gne noi- re, La fai-sait re-ten-tir de ses cris dou-lou-

[Basse continue]

-reux: A-che-vons, di-sait-il, mil-le ex-ploits a-mou-reux Que l'a-ve-nir ne puis-se

croi- re. Ô! Dul-ci-né-e, ô! toi, sour- ce de mes en-

-nuis, Di-vi-ne per-le de la Man-che, Beau so-leil de mes jours et lu-ne de mes nuits, Que de moments heureux ta rigueur me retranche.

[enchaîner]

3. [Air]

Très lentement

Loin des yeux qui m'ont fait captif, Je brûle d'une ardeur grégeoise; Jamais un penser lénitif N'allège mon âme pantoise,

88

Loin des yeux qui m'ont fait cap- tif, Je brû- le d'u- ne ar- deur gré- geoi- se;

Ja- mais un pen- ser lé- ni- tif N'al- lè- ge mon â- me pan- toi- se.

Fin

Cha- que jour je na- vre le cœur De main- te rei- ne lan- guis-

-san- te, Et je pré- fè- re à leur dou- ceur La cru- au- té de mon in- fan- te,

4. [Récitatif]

Désolons, ravageons cette forêt antique, Renversons ces rochers; mais non, je ferais mieux D'imiter d'Amadis la douleur pacifique. Surpassons, s'il se peut, de ce beau ténébreux L'incomparable péni-

-ten- ce: Cou- lez, mes pleurs, ga- rants de ma con-stance, I- non- dez ces dé- serts af- freux, Cou- lez, mes pleurs, ga--rants de ma con- stance, I- non- dez ces dé- serts af- freux. Et vous, ra- ce fé- lon- ne, à me nui- re oc-cu- pé- e, Gé- ants ou- tre-cui- dés, per- fi- des né- cro- mants, Je dé- po- se au jour--d'hui ma re- dou- ta- ble é- pé- e; Pour la pre- miè- re fois, goû- tez de doux mo- ments.

5. [Air]

-moi- re Des mi- ra- cles de mon ar- deur, Con- sa- crez l'il- lus- tre mé-

-moi- re Des mi- ra- cles de mon ar- deur.

Fin

N'ou- bli- ez pas dans mon his- toi- re Un seul in- stant de ce grand jour,

N'ou- bli- ez pas dans mon his- toi- re Un seul in- stant de ce grand

94

[Lyrics measures 25-30, Tenor:]
jour; Je vais don-ner à la vic- toi- re Le re-pos que m'ô- te l'a- mour, Je vais don-ner à la vic- -toi- re Le re- pos, _____ le re- pos que m'ô-te l'a- mour, Je vais don-ner à la vic-

[Measures 31-33, Tenor:]
-toi- re Le re- pos, _____ le re- pos que m'ô-te l'a- mour.

Comme ci-dessus 𝄋
jusqu'à la fin

6. Récitatif

[Taille:] Le fa- meux che- va- lier de la tris- te fi- gu- re Par ces fou- gueux trans-

-ports insultait la raison, Tandis que Rossinante, escorté du grison, Sur de maigres rochers dépouillés de verdure S'efforçait d'arracher un aride gazon. Là, le sobre Sancho, secondant son courage Par un reste de cervelas, À son large flacon livrait de doux combats, Et goûtait à longs traits un plus charmant breuvage Que le baume de Fierabras. Mais voyant son cher maître accablé de sa peine, De ses tendres chagrins entretenir les ours, Le fidèle écuy-

-er, la bouche en-co- re plei- ne, S'es-suy-a la mous- ta- che et lui tint ce dis- cours.

7. [Air]

Mar- di! __ faut- -il __ pour u- ne in- gra- te Pas- ser tant de nuits sans gra- bat? Pal- san- gué!

97

grat- tons qui nous grat- te, Au- tre- ment à bon chat bon rat, à bon chat bon rat. Le jeu ne vaut pas la chan- del- le, Vo- tre in- fan- te est u- ne gue- non; La sau- ce que l'on fait pour el- le Coû- te plus cher que le pois- son. Mar- di! faut- il pour u- ne in- gra- te Pas- ser tant

Fin

Comme ci-dessus 𝄋
jusqu'à la fin

Dom Quichote

Cantate françoise à une voix
avec grande simphonie

INSTRUMENTS

Flûte
Trompette
Violon
Vielle
Basson
Timbales
Basse continue

1. Prélude

2. Récitatif

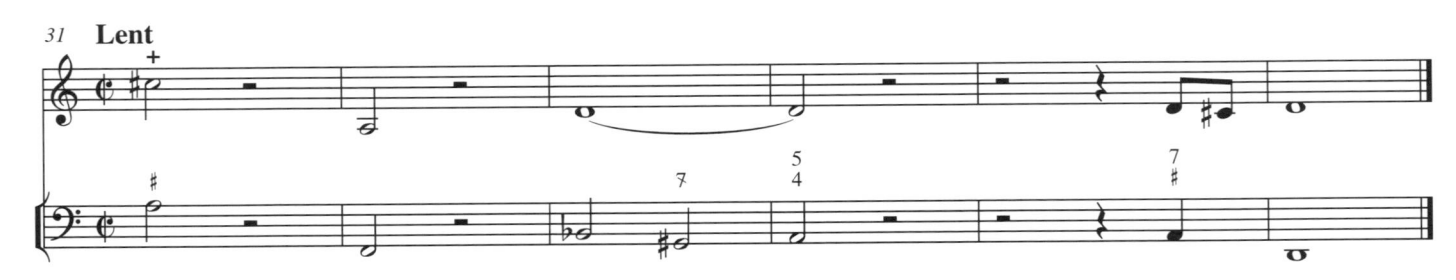

Lent

[Dessus] Dom Quichote, enfoncé dans la montagne noire, La faisait retentir de ses cris douloureux: Achevons, disait-il, mille exploits amoureux Que l'avenir ne puisse croire. Ô! Dulcinée! ô! toi, source de mes ennuis! Divine perle de la Manche, Beau soleil de mes jours et lune de mes nuits, Que de moments heureux ta rigueur me retranche.

[enchaîner]

3. Air

Fl.
Vn.
Bn.
D
B.c.
yeux qui m'ont fait cap- tif, Je brû- le d'u- ne ar- deur gré- geoi- se; Ja- mais un pen- ser lé- ni-
-tif N'al- lè- ge mon â- me pan- toi- se, Ja-
-mais un pen- ser lé- ni- tif N'al- lè- ge mon â- me pan- toi- se.
Fin

Cha- que jour je na- vre le cœur De main- te rei- ne lan- guis- san- te, Et je pré- fè- re à leur dou- ceur La cru- au- té de mon in- fan- te, Et je pré- fè- re à leur dou- ceur La cru- au-

4. Récitatif

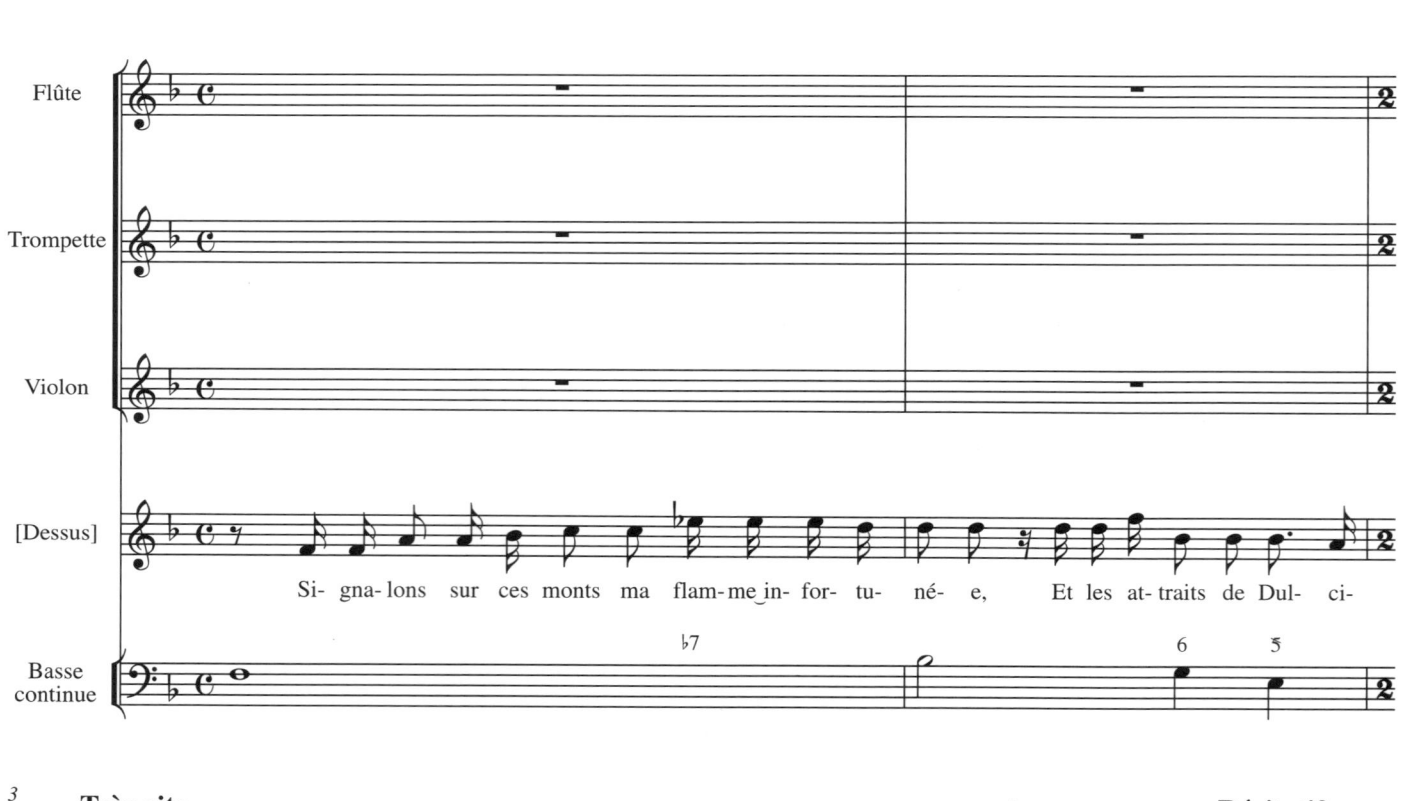

-té de mon infan- te. Loin des yeux qui m'ont fait cap- tif, Je brû- le

Comme ci-dessus 𝄋
jusqu'à la fin

Si- gna- lons sur ces monts ma flam-me in- for- tu- né- e, Et les at- traits de Dul- ci-

Très vite — **Récitatif**

-né- e. C'en est

107

fait, é-ga-lons les ef-forts fu-ri-eux Du ter-ri-ble a-mant d'An-gé-

Très vite

-li- que:

Récitatif **Très vite**

Dé-so-lons, ra-va-geons cet-te fo-rêt an- ti- que,

Récitatif

Ren-ver- sons ces ro-

Très vite

-chers;

108

Récitatif

mais non, je ferais mieux D'imiter d'Amadis la douleur pacifique. Surpassons, s'il se peut, de ce beau ténébreux L'incomparable pénitence: Coulez, mes pleurs, garants de ma constance, Inondez ces déserts af-

mesuré et lent

[mesuré et lent]

Lent et marqué

Tendrement

-freux, Cou- lez, mes pleurs, ga- rants de ma con- stan- ce, I- non- -dez ces dé- serts af- freux. Et vous, ra- ce fé- lon- ne, à me nui- re oc- cu- -pé- e, Gé- ants ou- tre- cui- dés, per- fi- des né- cro- mants, Je dé- po- se au- jour- d'hui

Récitatif

Mesuré

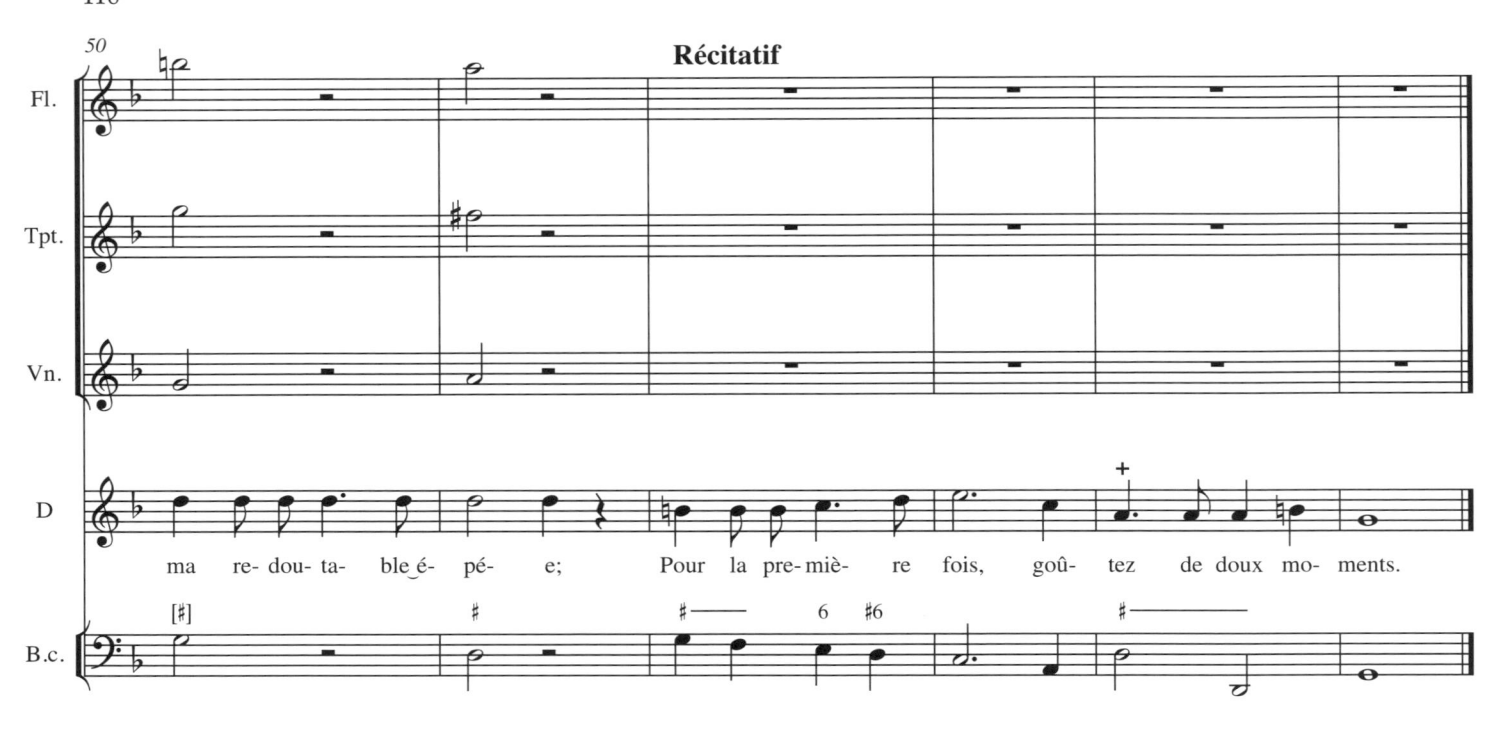

5. Air

Lyrics (Récitatif): ma re-dou-ta-ble é-pé-e; Pour la pre-miè-re fois, goû-tez de doux mo-ments.

Lyrics (Air): Vous, qui tra-vail-lez à ma gloi-

8
Tpt.
Vn.
D
- re, Ve-nez, vo- lez, sa-ge‿en- chan- teur; Con- sa- crez l'il- lus- tre mé-
B.c.
Timb.
12
-moi- re Des mi- ra- cles de mon ar- deur,
16
Vous, qui tra-vail- lez à ma gloi- - re, Ve- nez, vo- lez, vo-

20
Tpt.
Vn.
D
-lez, sa- ge en- chan- teur; Con- sa- crez l'il- lus- tre mé- moi- re Des mi-
B.c.
Timb.
25
Tpt.
Vn.
D
-ra- cles de mon ar- deur, Con- sa- crez l'il- lus- tre mé-
B.c.
Timb.
30
Tpt.
Vn.
D
-moi- re Des mi- ra- cles de mon ar- deur.
B.c.
Timb.
[3]

113

-stant de ce grand jour; Je vais don- ner à la vic- toi- re Le re-pos que m'ô- te l'a- mour, Je vais don- ner à la vic- toi- re Le re-pos que m'ô- te l'a- mour, Je vais don- ner à la vic- toi- re Le re- pos, le re- pos que m'ô- te l'a- mour.

Comme ci-dessus 𝄋
jusqu'à la fin

6. Récitatif

Le fa- meux Che- va- lier de la tris- te fi- gu- re Par ces fou- gueux trans- ports in- sul- tait la rai- son, Tan- dis que Ros- si- nan- te, es- cor- té du gri- son, Sur de mai- gres ro- chers dé- pouil- lés de ver- du- re S'ef- for- çait d'ar- ra- cher un a- ri- de ga- zon. San- cho, dans ce dé- sert sau- va- ge, Peu tou- ché de leur em- bar- ras, À son lar- ge fla- con li- vrait de doux com-

116

-bats, Et goû-tait à longs traits un plus char-mant breu-va-ge Que le bau-me de Fie-ra-bras. Mais d'un maî-tre ché-

-ri la tris-tes-se fa-ta-le De ses plai-sirs in-ter-rom-pit le cours; Le fi-dè-le_é-cuy-

-er, rap-pe-lant sa mo-ra-le, Au ten-dre Dom Qui-cho-t[e]_a-dres-sa ce dis-cours.

7. Air

Vielle

[Dessus]

Basse continue

Ve.

D

B.c.

Ve.
D
B.c.
Mor- di! faut- il pour u- ne in- gra- te Pas- ser tant de nuits sans gra- bat?
Pal- san- gué! grat- tons qui nous grat- te, Au- tre- ment à bon chat bon
rat, à bon chat bon
rat.
Fin
Le jeu ne vaut pas la chan-

-del- le, Vo-tre in-fan- te est u- ne gue- non; La sau- ce que l'on fait pour

el- le Coû- te plus cher que le pois- son.

Comme ci-dessus 𝄋
jusqu'à la fin

Critical Report

Sigla

D-8466	Paris, Bibliothèque nationale de France, D-8466 (2)
MUS 293	Paris, Bibliothèque de l'Arsenal, MUS 293
S 120/8000	Stuttgart, Württembergische Landesbibliothek, S 120/8000
Vm7-162	Paris, Bibliothèque nationale de France, Vm7-162
Vm7-163	Paris, Bibliothèque nationale de France, Vm7-163
Vm7-440	Paris, Bibliothèque nationale de France, Vm7-440
X-644	Paris, Bibliothèque nationale de France, X-644 (1)

Sources

The primary source for most of Courbois's cantatas is the engraved edition of 1710. Four exemplars survive, all with slightly different title pages: Vm7-162, MUS 293, S 120/8000, and D-8466.[1] Their respective title pages read as follows:

Vm7-162: CANTATES | FRANÇOISES | à I. et II. voix. | *Sans Simphonie et avec Simphonie.* | DÉDIÉES | A SON ALTESSE SÉRÉNISSIME | MADAME LA DUCHESSE DU MAINE | Composées | PAR LE SIEUR COURBOIS. | les Paroles sont de MONS.^ieur FUZELLIER. | *Gravées par CLAUDE ROUSSEL* | [brace] Prix broché 5.₶10f | Et Relié en Veau 7.₶ | A PARIS | Se Vend Chez [brace] *l'AUTEUR, ruë S^T. Antoine, chez M^r. De la Jarye Comm.^re* | FOUCAUT, *ruë S^T. Honoré, à la Règle d'Or.* | AVEC PRIVILÈGE DU ROY. 1710.

MUS 293: CANTATES | FRANÇOISES | à I. et II. voix. | *Sans Simphonie et avec Simphonie.* | DÉDIÉES | A SON ALTESSE SÉRÉNISSIME | MADAME LA DUCHESSE DU MAINE | Composées | PAR LE SIEUR COURBOIS. | les Paroles sont de MONS.^ieur FUZELLIER. | *Gravées par CLAUDE ROUSSEL* | [brace] Prix broché 5.₶10f 6₶ | Et Relié en Veau 7.₶ 8.₶10 | A PARIS | Se Vend Chez [brace] *l'AUTEUR, ruë S^T. Antoine, chez M^r. De la Jarye Comm.^re* | FOUCAUT, *ruë S^T. Honoré, à la Règle d'Or.* | AVEC PRIVILÈGE DU ROY. 1710.

S 120/8000: CANTATES | FRANÇOISES | à I. et II. voix. | *Sans Simphonie et avec Simphonie.* | DÉDIÉES | A SON ALTESSE SÉRÉNISSIME | MADAME LA DUCHESSE DU MAINE | Composées | PAR LE SIEUR COURBOIS. | les Paroles sont de MONS.^ieur FUZELLIER. | *Gravées par CLAUDE ROUSSEL.* | [brace] Prix broché 6.₶ | 3.e Edition. | A PARIS | Se Vend Chez [brace] *l'AUTEUR, ruë S^T. Antoine, chez M^r. De la Jarye Comm.^re* | FOUCAUT, *ruë S^T. Honoré, à la Règle d'Or.* | AVEC PRIVILÈGE DU ROY. 1710.

D-8466: CANTATES | FRANÇOISES | à I. et II. voix. | *Sans Simphonie et avec Simphonie.* | DÉDIÉES | A SON ALTESSE SÉRÉNISSIME | MADAME LA DUCHESSE DU MAINE | Composées | PAR LE SIEUR COURBOIS. | les Paroles sont de MONS.^ieur FUZELLIER. | *Gravées par CLAUDE ROUSSEL.* | Prix broché 7.₶ | 4e. Edition. | A PARIS | Se Vend Chez [brace] *l'AUTEUR, ruë S^T. Antoine, chez M^r. De la Jarye Comm.^re* | FOUCAUT, *ruë S^T. Honoré, à la Règle d'Or.* | AVEC PRIVILÈGE DU ROY. 1710.

The colophon at the end of each exemplar reads "FIN | Gravé par C. Roussel. 1710."

The appearance of "3.e Edition" and "4.e Edition" on the title pages of S 120/8000 and D-8466 suggest that at least four versions of the book were issued. Although no edition numbers are shown on the other two exemplars, the progressively rising prices on all four title pages suggest that Vm7-162 may have been the first edition and MUS 293 (on whose title page the old price of the first edition has been crossed out by hand) the second. Also supporting this hypothesis is the fact that D-8466, MUS 293, and S 120/8000 are made from identical plates and incorporate several changes and corrections to errors in Vm7-162, particularly in the basse continue part, which includes more detailed figures in the later editions.

The present edition is based on D-8466 (see plate 1) in order to incorporate the changes, corrections, and additions made after the publication of the first edition. Due to the occasional lack of clarity in this source, MUS 293 and S 120/8000—the presumed second edition and the third edition—have been consulted as concordant sources. Vm7-162 has been consulted in order to clarify uncertain cases in the bass figures and to note the occasional changes made by Courbois in the basse continue part. To avoid unnecessary clutter, however, only the most significant variants have been detailed in the critical notes. Changes and corrections to the bass figures between the first and subsequent editions have not been listed in most cases.

A few additional sources contain individual cantatas by Courbois from the 1710 publication. A handwritten copy of *Dom Quichote* (no. 7), dated 1718 and prepared by a certain Joubert de Corbeville (first name unknown), is housed in the Bibliothèque nationale de France under the shelfmark Ms Vm7-4769; it bears the title "Dom Quichote De La Manche, Cantate VIIe, A une voix Et Un Violon, par M^r. Courbois." *Jason et Médée* (no. 6) appears in an undated manuscript copy in the library of the Conservatorio di Santa Cecilia in Rome under the shelfmark A.Ms.3978 (RISM A/II No. 850.041.217), which bears the heading "MÉDÉE ET JASON | Cantate a deux voix." Finally, the print Vm7-440 contains the 1710 version of *Dom Quichote* in incomplete form; this print, which lacks a frontispiece and the first two pages of music, has been miscataloged as the later version for *grande symphonie*, yet it is clearly the chamber version for voice and obbligato instruments. A second and complete exemplar of Vm7-440 is housed in The British Library, H.346.d.(2.) (RISM A/I/2/ No. C 4317). The title page reads as follows and clearly identifies Jean-Pantaléon Le Clerc as the publisher:

DOMGUICHOTE | CANTATE | *A Voix Seul* | *Avec Simphonie.* | PAR | M^R. Courbois | Prix 2^{tt}. 8^s. | *La Simphonie du Violon, tirez Separement 12^s.* | [rule] | A PARIS | *Chez Le Sieur Le Clerc Rüe du Roule a la Croix d'Or.*

This source is clearly based on Vm7-162, although different plates have been used. The music is identical to that of Vm7-162 with the exception of a few added ornaments and tempo labels. Its precise use of tempo labels and its prescriptive practice towards ornaments suggests that it may be a later print (no date is shown on the title page, though the British Library catalog dates it around 1740). These additional sources include few significant differences from the 1710 print, though individual exceptions are discussed below in the critical notes.

The primary source for the *grande symphonie* version of *Dom Quichote* (ca. 1728) is an undated engraved edition surviving in two identical exemplars in the Bibliothèque nationale (Vm7-163; X-644; see plate 5):

DOM QUICHOTE | Cantate Françoise | a vne Voix | Avec grande Simphonie | Composées | PAR | M^R. Courbois | *Les paroles sont de M^r. Fuzelier.* | Le prix 3. ₶ | [ornament] Gravé p. L. Hue | A PARIS | Au Mont Parnasse | Chez [brace] L'Auteur rüe Fromanteau. | Le S^r. Boivin rüe S^t. Honoré à la Regle d'Or. | Le S^r. Le Clair rüe du Roule a la Croix d'Or. | Avec Privilege du Roy.

Vm7-163 was consulted as the primary source for this edition since it is the clearer of the two.

With the exception of *Orphée, Ariane,* and *Dom Quichote,* the texts of Courbois's cantatas, which are all by Louis Fuzelier, survive solely in the above musical sources. Fuzelier's text for *Ariane* was also set by Jean-Baptiste Stuck (also known as Battistin) in his second collection of *Cantates françoises* (1708) with some minor textual variants (not listed in the critical notes).[2] *Orphée* was also set by Antonio Guido (1710–11, incomplete) and by a certain Lacroix (ca. 1714–30); both settings contain textual variants not listed in the critical notes.[3] The version of *Ariane* set by Stuck and the text to *Dom Quichote* (the latter also with minor variants not reported in the critical notes) appear in the most important cantata text anthology of the period, Jean Bachelier's *Recueil de cantates* (The Hague, 1728), whose title page reads as follows:

RECUEIL | de | CANTATES | Contenant toutes celles qui se chantent | dans les Concerts: pour l'usage des Amateurs de la Musique & de la Poësie. | par J. BACHELIER, *Maître* | *de la Musique à la Haye.* | [illustration] | A LA HAYE, | Chez ALBERTS & vander KLOOT. | [rule] | MDCCXXVIII.

Ariane appears on pages 56–59 with the heading "XVIII. | ARIANE. | Cantate à voix seule, & Basse continue. | *Les Paroles sont de Mr. . . . .* | *La Musique de Mr. Batistin.*" *Dom Quichote* appears on pages 221–24, with the heading "LVIX. | DON-QUICHOTTE. | Cantate Burlesque à voix seule, avec ac- | compagnement. | *Les Paroles sont de Mr. K.* | *La Musique de Mr. B.*" The identity of "Mr. K." is unknown, although it is unclear why Bachelier would disguise the identity of Fuzelier, otherwise clearly identified as the author of the text to *Dom Quichote* in all the Courbois sources. However, in the index of his *Recueil de cantates* (under the heading *Don Quichotte*), Bachelier reveals the identity of "Mr. B" as Thomas-Louis Bourgeois. While no such setting by Bourgeois is known to exist,[4] an anonymous and thus far unattributed French cantata setting of this version of Fuzelier's *Dom Quichote,* for haute-contre, violin, and continuo, was published in the March and April 1711 installments of Estienne Roger's *Recueil d'airs sérieux et à boire de différents autheurs.*[5] Further study and a systematic stylistic analysis of Bourgeois's cantatas—well beyond the scope of the present study—would be necessary before attributing the setting in Roger's publication to Bourgeois. In any case, it is unclear why Bourgeois, already well-established as a composer of cantatas and theatrical works, would choose to publish a cantata anonymously outside France, especially since all of his known works were published in Paris.[6] Whatever the case may be, the anonymous setting of Fuzelier's *Dom Quichote* in Roger's *Recueil* shows that at least one other composer besides Courbois set this text.

Editorial Methods

The numbering and titles of the cantatas from *Cantates françoises à I et II voix* are based on those given in that source, with spelling and accents modernized, abbreviations tacitly expanded, and periods at the end of words or lines tacitly omitted. Movement titles have been preserved from the sources unless absent, in which case they have been supplied in brackets. Movement numbers have been added editorially before each movement title.

Throughout the edition, score order has been regularized so that all obbligato instruments are placed above the vocal line. One exception can be found in the fifth movement of the 1728 version of *Dom Quichote* ("Vous, qui travaillez à ma gloire"), where the basse continue and the timpani share a staff, as in the source (see plate 6). The occasional appearance of basse continue figures above some timpani notes in this movement (not shown in plate 6) suggest that the latter could be taken by a bass viol or other continuo instrument if necessary.

All textual elements from the source have been standardized in the edition, including tempo markings, section labels, designations of vocal and instrumental parts, and written instructions; their placement and alignment have been regularized. The labels of vocal parts have been added editorially (in brackets) based on the cleffing of the parts. The edition retains the French names of instrumental parts when they are given in the source, with one exception: plural labels that indicate more than one instrument playing in unison (see "Notes on Performance" in the introduction) have been changed from plural to singular, with the original part name given in the critical notes. The violin part in *Orphée* (no. 4), labeled "Violons" in the source, is labeled "Violon 1, 2" in the edition to account for the divisi in the opening movement (see plate 3). The *vielle* in the final movement of both versions of *Dom Quichote* is a hurdy-gurdy with chanters in D and drones in G and D (Bourbonnais tuning). In *Jason et Médée* (no. 6), the character designations "Jason" and "Médée" are not given consistently in the source; they have been added tacitly to the edition where appropriate. Tempo and expression markings follow the sources, with orthography modernized as necessary. Certain labels in the sources, such as *tendrement* or *légèrement*, denote both tempo and expression; since they are usually found at the beginning of new sections or movements, their tempo connotation has been privileged in the edition. All textual elements in brackets have been added editorially.

Clefs have been modernized according to current usage. Vocal parts originally in C1 clef and instrumental parts originally in G1 clef have been transcribed in treble clef, and vocal parts originally in C3 clef (as in *L'Amant timide*) or C4 clef (as in the 1710 version of *Dom Quichote*) are transcribed in transposing treble clef. F4 clef is employed for basse-taille vocal parts (as in *Orphée* and the part of Jason in *Jason et Médée*), basse continue, and bassoon, and is retained in the edition. Some higher basse continue passages are notated in C3 and C4 in the source; such passages have been transcribed in either treble or bass clef as appropriate.

In general, the edition maintains the text underlay of the sources; exceptions are indicated in the critical notes. The punctuation and orthography of the sources have been tacitly modernized and all abbreviations have been expanded. First letters of poetic lines have been capitalized regardless of their appearance in the sources; were text is repeated, however, this capitalization is maintained only for the repetition of entire poetic lines. Commas are added where necessary to clarify text repetition. Word division follows modern French practice. Any added text is placed in brackets.

In most cases, this edition retains the time signatures and key signatures of the sources; any editorial changes to these elements are discussed on a case-by-case basis in the critical notes. A time signature of **3** is generally equivalent to the modern ¾, and both **2** and ¢ are used to indicate a duple meter with two half notes (or equivalent) per measure. The key signatures of the source include some obsolete modal signatures (such as two flats for C minor with the third flat added as an accidental when needed), which are retained in the edition. Since the early eighteenth century was still a time of transition, cases can be found in which composers used a modern key signature but signed some individual notes with accidentals already in that signature (e.g., A♭ in C minor with a three-flat signature). Redundant accidentals arising from this situation have been omitted without comment. Where necessary, key signatures have been modernized to eliminate archaisms and redundancies (such as the signing of F♯ in two octaves).

Barlines in the edition follow those of the sources. Double barlines are used inconsistently in the sources to delineate sections, especially in dal segno arias; they have been retained or added as needed. In some such arias, the final measure of the B section is incomplete in order to correspond with a segno in the middle of an earlier measure. These incomplete final measures have been filled tacitly, double barlines have been added, and the corresponding segnos have been repositioned accordingly. Modern final barlines are used at the end of movements that do not involve dal segno or da capo repeats.

The notation of repeats and subsequent endings is inconsistent in the sources and has been standardized in the edition to conform to modern practice. Verbal repeat instructions are phrased variously in the source of 1710 and have been standardized to "Comme ci-dessus ℅ jusqu'à la fin" (indicating a return to the measure marked with a segno). In the *grande symphonie* version of *Dom Quichote*, the Italian label "Da Capo" appears in the source at the end of the fifth and seventh movements, though both movements require a return to a measure other than the first. For these movements, the edition adopts the standardized wording "Comme ci-dessus ℅ jusqu'à la fin," but specifies the original version in the critical notes.

Modern practice for stem direction and beaming is employed throughout the edition in both vocal and instrumental parts, which does not differ greatly from the original source. Slurs indicating vocal melismas in the source have been omitted without comment, while slurs denoting the extension of a harmony in the basse continue have been modernized to extender lines. Tied notes within a measure sometimes occur in the source when a measure is split across two systems, though a few occur in unsplit measures for no apparent reason. Such tied notes have been tacitly replaced in the edition by a single note of their combined value, except if their combined value conflicts with the correct length of the measure; exceptions of this sort are cited in the critical notes. Editorial slurs and ties are dashed.

The note and rest values of the sources have been transcribed in a 1:1 ratio, with some tacit adjustments made to the visual presentation of rests. Other adjustments to source rhythmic values are discussed on a case-by-case basis in the critical notes. Editorially added notes and rests appear in brackets.

Following modern practice, accidentals are assumed to be valid through the end of the measure. Redundant source accidentals have been eliminated without comment, though some cautionary accidentals from the source have been retained when they are deemed potentially useful to performers. Accidentals added by the editor are placed in brackets; editorial cautionary accidentals are enclosed in parentheses. In cases where an editorial accidental precedes a source accidental in the same measure, the source accidental has been removed without comment. For the most part, the 1710 source employs only two symbols for accidentals: flats to lower pitches by half step (also used to change sharps to naturals) and sharps to raise them by half step (also used to change flats to naturals and change sharps to double sharps); natural signs are used occasionally to raise notes by a half step. Where necessary, such signs have been changed to their modern equivalents with no further indication in the critical notes.

The ornaments and articulation markings of the source (see "Notes on Performance" in the introduction) are retained in the edition, with the following slight differences in presentation. Zigzag trill signs (see plate 2), representing the *tremblement feint* described by Montéclair, have been modernized as unslashed mordents. Wavy, slur-like curves are used in the sources to indicate both the *enflé* bowstroke and the vibrato-based techniques of *flaté* and *balancement;* the edition uses trill extension lines to indicate the vibrato techniques and modern crescendo wedges for *enflé*. Ornamental signs in all parts except the basse continue are placed above the staff, regardless of where they occur in the source; ornaments in the basse continue part are placed below the staff. Various note values are used for appoggiaturas in the source, although it is unknown whether or not this signifies any difference in execution; the original values have been retained in this edition. The placement of ornaments and articulation markings in relation to the notes they affect, which is sometimes inconsistent in the sources, has been regularized in the edition.

Basse continue figures are original, even when ♯ or ♭ is equivalent to ♮ in modern practice. All figures are notated above the staff, regardless of where they appear in the source; the same is true for the figures above the timpani notes in the fifth movement of the second version of *Dom Quichote*. Figures are placed metrically to correspond to the indicated harmonic changes and are stacked from highest to lowest in conformance with modern practice. Accidentals that follow a figure in the source have been placed before the figure in the edition. Slashed figures, which denote diminished intervals in the source, have been retained; the use of the letter *x* to denote ♯ preceding or following a figure has been tacitly changed to ♯. Editorial figures or accidental symbols have been placed in brackets.

Critical Notes

The critical notes record title information from the primary sources, rejected source readings that are not otherwise covered in the editorial methods, and, where necessary, significant variants from other editions of Courbois's *Cantates françoises à I et II voix*. The following abbreviations are used: Fl. = Flûte, Tpt. = Trompette, Vn. = Violon, Bn. = Basson, D = Dessus, HC = Haute-contre, T = Taille, BT= Basse-taille, Jas. = Jason, Méd. = Médée, B.c.= Basse continue, Timb. = Timbales. Notes and chords are counted consecutively within a measure, with tied, bracketed, and ornamental elements included in the count. Rests, including bracketed rests, are counted separately. Pitches are identified according to the system in which c' denotes middle C.

Cantates françoises à I et II voix

If no siglum is cited in the notes below, then the reading is from the primary source (D-8466). Variant readings identify the concordant source as part of the critical note.

No. 1. Apollon et Daphné

Title. Apollon | et | Daphné. | 1ere Cantate | *à voix seule*

1. Récitatif. M. 20, B.c., time signature is **2**.

2. Air. M. 29, B.c., note 3, figure is 9. M. 44, B.c., beats 1–2, extender line moved from beats 3–4. M. 53, B.c., beats 1–2, extender line moved from beats 3–4. M. 61, D, notes 3–6 are 16th–dotted 8th–16th–dotted 8th in Vm7-162. M. 62, D, notes 1–4 are 16th–dotted 8th–16th–dotted 8th in Vm7-162; B.c., note 3 has figure $\frac{5}{4}$. M. 66, B.c., beats 1–2, extender line moved from beats 3–4. M. 71, B.c., beats 3–4 have extender line. M. 72, B.c., note 5, figure is $\frac{5}{4}$.

4. Air. M. 31, B.c., notes 2–4 are all g in Vm7-162. M. 41, B.c., beat 3 has extender line.

5. Récitatif. M. 8, D, notes 9–10, syllables "-le aux" moved from notes 8–9.

6. [Mesuré]. M. 17, B.c., note 2, figures are $\frac{6}{5}$ above staff, 4 below. M. 18, B.c., note 1, figure is $\frac{5}{4}$.

7. Air. M. 4, B.c., note 11, figure is ♯3. M. 12, B.c., note 9, figure is $\frac{5}{4}$. M. 14, D, note 7, + moved from note 9. M. 21, B.c., note 1 is lacking in Vm7-162.

No. 2. Zéphire et Flore

Title. Zéphire | et | Flore. | II.e Cantate. | *a voix seule.*

1. [Récitatif]. M. 2, D, note 2 is dotted quarter in Vm7-162. M. 5, D, notes 4–5 are both quarters in Vm7-162. M. 20, B.c., note 3 lacks sharp in Vm7-162; note 4, figure is ♯3. M. 21, B.c., note 18 is d♯ in Vm7-162. M. 26, D, note 7 lacks sharp in Vm7-162.

2. Air. M. 3, B.c., rest 1 is 8th; note 3 is 8th. M. 9, B.c., note 1 is quarter. M. 25, B.c., note 4 lacks flat in Vm7-162. M. 43, B.c., rest 2 is missing; double barline moved from end of m. 42; part labeled "reprise." M. 52, B.c., note 2 lacks sharp in Vm7-162. M. 62, B.c., note 5 is d 16th–e 16th in Vm7-162. M. 68, D, notes 1–2 are dotted 8th–16th in Vm7-162.

3. Récitatif. M. 11, B.c. is g quarter–f quarter–e half in Vm7-162.

4. Air. M. 1, B.c., meter is $\frac{3}{9}$. M. 14, D, note 1 is quarter, note 3 is dotted quarter; edition follows Vm7-162. M. 28, B.c., slur is between notes 4–5.

5. Récitatif. M. 21, B.c., note 4, figure is 3.

6. Air. M. 18, D, notes 2–4 are all 16ths. M. 20, B.c., note 5, figure is ♯3. M. 26, B.c., note 5, figure is ♯3. M. 35, B.c., note 2, part labeled "reprise." M. 36, B.c., notes 3–4 are not slurred in Vm-162. M. 39, B.c. notes 3–4 are not slurred in Vm-162. M. 40, B.c., notes 1–2 are not slurred in Vm-162. M. 43, B.c., notes 1–2 are not slurred in Vm-162. M. 44, B.c., notes 1–2 are not slurred in Vm-162. M. 56, D, notes 5–7 are 16th–8th–16th.

No. 3. L'Amant timide

Title. l'Amant timide | IIIme Cantate | *à voix seule.*

1. Récitatif. M. 3, B.c., notes 2–3 are A quarter in Vm7-162. M. 7, HC, notes 5–6 are both quarters in Vm7-162. M. 15, B.c., note 2 is d quarter with figure ♮ in Vm7-162, notes 3–4 are half note e♭ with figures 4♯–3–6 in Vm7-162. M. 19, HC, note 1 lacks flat in Vm7-162.

2. Air. M. 34, HC is g' half–quarter rest–f' quarter in Vm7-162.

3. Récitatif. M. 10, HC, note 1 is dotted quarter in Vm7-162; note 5 is 8th in Vm7-162.

4. Air. M. 9, B.c., note 12, figure is ♯3. M. 16, B.c., note 10 has figure ♭. M. 17, HC, notes 7–9 are d' 8th–d' 16th–c' 16th in Vm7-162. M. 26, B.c., note 11 has figure 3. M. 33, B.c., notes 3–5 are g–f–e in Vm7-162. M. 36, B.c., note 9, figure 8 moved from note 8. M. 37, B.c., note 9, figure 6 moved from note 8. M. 38, note 8, figure 8 moved from note 7.

6. Air. M. 1, B.c. has erroneous segno, meter is $^6_8$; HC, time signature is lacking. M. 4, B.c., slur spans notes 1–3. M. 8, HC, notes 1–2 are dotted 8th–16th. M. 17, B.c., notes 1–2 are both 8ths. M. 18, B.c., notes 4–5 are slurred. M. 19, B.c., notes 1–2 are both 8ths. M. 26, HC, notes 2–3 are both 8ths. M. 27, repeat sign moved from m. 26, note 1. M. 33, B.c., notes 2–3 are both g. M. 34, B.c., note 1 is c♯', note 2 is d', note 3 is c♯', notes 4–5 are both c♯'.

No. 4. Orphée

Title. Orphée. | IIIIE Cantate | *à voix seule et un Violon.*

1. [Récitatif]. M. 1, Vn. 1, 2, part labeled "Violons." M. 28, Vn. 1, 2, dyad, lower note lacks dot; B.c., note 1 is d half–quarter rest. M. 44, B.c., note 1 lacks natural in Vm7-162. M. 55, B.c., erroneous cautionary bass clef. M. 64, B.c., note 5, figure moved from note 7. M. 72, B.c., note 3 is G♮ in Vm7-162. M. 73, B.c., note 5, figure moved from note 7. M. 83, B.c., note 5, figure moved from note 7. M. 86, B.c., note 11, figure moved from note 12. M. 87, BT and B.c., note is whole.

2. [Air]. M. 1, Vn. 1, 2, part labeled "Violons." M. 5, B.c., note 2 has figure 3. M. 13, B.c., beat 1, figure is $^5_4$. M. 26, B.c., notes 1–3 are slurred. M. 47, BT, note 1 is quarter. M. 60, Vn. 1, 2, notes 1–2 are f' dotted quarter–g' 16th–a' 16th–g' 16th (with the three 16ths forming a triplet) in Vm7-162. M. 75, B.c., note 1, figure is $^6_{♯4}$.

4. Air. M. 60, BT, ornament (+) lacking; edition follows Vm7-162. M. 68, B.c., beat 3, figure is ♯3. M. 78, B.c., beat 3, figure is ♯3. Mm. 82–83, Tpt., notes have tie in Vm7-162. M. 86, BT, note 3 is quarter note–8th rest. M. 98, B.c., rest is half. M. 125, B.c., note 3, figure is 5♯. M. 126, B.c., note 3, figure is ♯3.

6. Air. M. 1, Vn. 1, 2, part labeled "Violons." M. 4, Vn. 1, 2, slur spans notes 5–7. M. 10, BT, notes 7–8 are both 8ths in Vm7-162. M. 12, BT, notes 5–6 are both 8ths in Vm7-162. M. 13, BT, notes 7–8 are both 8ths in Vm7-162. M. 15, B.c., notes 3–4 are not slurred, notes 6–7 are not slurred; edition follows Vm7-162. M. 29, B.c., notes 5–6 are not slurred in Vm7-162; Vn. 1, 2, notes 5–6, slur moved from notes 6–7.

No. 5. Ariane

Title. Ariane | v.^{E} Cantate | à voix seul | *et un Violon.*

1. Récitatif. M. 10, D, note 1 lacks augmentation dot. M. 14, B.c., beat 2, figure is ♯4.

2. [Air]. M. 1, Vn., part labeled "Violons."

3. Récitatif. M. 3, B.c., notes 1–2 have figures 6 and 7, respectively, with extender line between them; Vm7-162 lacks figures but has extender between notes 1 and 2. M. 10, B.c. is half note tied to whole note. M. 14, B.c., note 3 is e quarter with no figure in Vm7-162. M. 15, B.c. is d♯ quarter (figure 6)–G♯ quarter (no figure)–D♯ half (figures $^5_4$–♯) in Vm7-162. M. 16, B.c., note 1, figure is ♯3.

4. [Air]. M. 25, Vn., bow vibrato and trill marks lacking; edition follows Vm7-162. M. 30, B.c., note 7, figure 3 moved from note 5. M. 32, Vn., beats 1–2 are quarter rest–8th rest–g" 8th; edition follows Vm7-162. Mm. 50–71, Vn., erroneous G2 clef. M. 58, B.c., note 9, figure ♯ moved from note 15. M. 66, Vn., note 9 is dotted half. M. 68, Vn., note 1 is dotted half, rest 1 is lacking in Vm7-162. M. 70, Vn., note 1 has "4" above in Vm7-162.

5. Récitatif. M. 2, D, notes 2, 3, 5, and 6 are all quarter notes; edition follows Vm7-162. M. 20, D, rest 1 is 8th; note 2 is quarter.

6. Air. M. 1, Vn., part labeled "Violons." M. 29, B.c., note 5 is 16th. M. 82, B.c., notes 4–5, slur moved from notes 5–6. M. 89, D, notes 1–2 are both 8ths; B.c., notes 2–3 are both 8ths.

No. 6. Jason et Médée

Title. Jason et Médée | vi.^{e} Cantate. | *à deux voix.*

1. [Récitatif]. M. 9, B.c., beat 3, figure is $^6_4$; edition follows Vm7-162.

2. [Duo]. M. 19, B.c., note 3 has figure 3. M. 22, B.c., note 3 has figure 3. M. 25, Méd., note 3, augmentation dot to left of notehead. M. 31, B.c., note 3 has figure 3. M. 43, B.c., note 3 has figure 3. M. 48, B.c., note 1 is c in Vm7-162. M. 49, B.c., note 3 has figure 3; note 4 is C. M. 52, B.c., note 3 has figure ♯3. M. 55, B.c., note 3 has figure 3; note 4 is B♭ (edition follows Vm7-162). M. 59,

B.c., note 3, figure is *o,* which may be the lower part of a figure 6; edition follows Vm7-162. M. 60, B.c., note 1, figure is $^5_4$; note 2 is D.

3. Récitatif. Label "Récitatif" lacking; edition follows Vm7-162. M. 19, B.c, note 1 has figure ♯.

4. Air. M. 8, B.c., note 9, figure is $^5_4$. M. 14, B.c., note 9, figure is $^5_4$. M. 25, Méd., rests 1–3 are two half rests. M. 29, Méd., note 3 is g″.

5. Récitatif. M. 13, Méd., B.c., note is half.

6. Air. M. 18, Jas., note 9 is dotted quarter. M. 20, B.c., extender (notated as slur) over notes 9–10; edition follows Vm7-162. M. 25, B.c, note 8, figure moved from note 5.

7. Récitatif. Mm. 1–3, B.c., ties are lacking in Vm7-162. M. 14, B.c., note 2, figure is $^6_{\flat}$. M. 16, B.c., beat 1, figure is $^6_{\flat}$; beat 4, figure is ♯3. M. 19, B.c. is e half (figure 6) tied to e half (figure 5); edition follows Vm7-162.

8. [Duo]. M. 3, B.c., note 3 is B₁. M. 10, B.c., note 3, figure is $^7_{\sharp 3}$. M. 101, B.c, beat 2, figure is $^6_{\sharp}$. M. 119, label "Fin."

No. 7. Dom Quichote

Title. Dom Quichote | VII.ᴱ CANTATE. | *à voix seule et un Violon.*

1. Prélude. M. 5, Vn., rest lacks augmentation dot; B.c., rest 3 lacks augmentation dot. M. 7, B.c., rest is quarter rest–16th rest; Vn., rest is 16th. M. 16, Vn., rest 2 is 16th. M. 17, B.c., rest 2.

3. [Air]. M. 3, Vn., rest 1 is quarter. M. 16, Vn., rest 3 lacks augmentation dot.

4. [Récitatif]. M. 1, T, note 4 is 8th. M. 2, T, note 6 is dotted 8th, rest 2 is lacking; edition follows Vm7-440.

M. 6, T, note 7 is quarter, notes 8–9 are both 8ths; edition follows Vm7-162. M. 7, B.c., note 5, second figure is ♯3. M. 11, T, notes 1–2 are 8ths. M. 12, T, note 2 is f′; edition follows Vm7-162. M. 14, B.c., beats 1–2 are half rest. M. 35, B.c., second figure is $^5_{\sharp 3}$.

5. [Air]. M. 1, Tpt, note 1 is dotted 16th. M. 4, T, note 1 is dotted 16th. M. 5, Tpt., note 1 is dotted 16th. M. 6, B.c., note 2 is dotted 16th. M. 7, T, note 5 is 16th. M. 8, Tpt, note 2 is dotted 16th. M. 9, T, note 1 is dotted 16th. M. 27, T, notes 7–8, text is "ta" instead of "la." M. 28, T, note 5 is dotted half, with beat 1 empty in m. 29. The augmentation dot has been altered by hand to quarter rest; edition follows Vm7-162. M. 31, T, note 5 is dotted half, with beat 1 empty in m. 32. The augmentation dot has been altered by hand to quarter rest; edition follows Vm7-162. M. 33, Tpt., note 1 is dotted 16th.

6. Récitatif. M. 23, B.c., note 2, figure is ♭3. M. 24, B.c., note 1, figure is ♭3.

7. [Air]. M. 36, B.c., chord 3, figure is $^6_4$.

Dom Quichote (ca. 1728)

1. Prélude. M. 1, Vn., part labeled "Violons." M. 2, Vn., extra quarter rest between note 1 and rest 1.

3. Air. M. 1, Fl., part labeled "Flûtes"; Vn., part labeled "Violons"; Bn., part labeled "Bassons."

4. Récitatif. M. 1, Fl., part labeled "Flûtes"; Vn., part labeled "Violons." M. 10, Vn., notes 3–4 are b♯′–c♯″; notes 7–8 are f″–g″. M. 27, meter is ₵. M. 52, B.c., note 1, figure is ♮.

5. Air. M. 1, Vn., part labeled "Violons." M. 2, segno lacking. M. 64, B.c./Timb., downstems lacking.

Notes

1. S 120/8000 is the basis for Philippe Courbois and Thomas-Louis Bourgeois, *Cantatas,* ed. David Tunley, Eighteenth-Century French Cantata, vol. 14 (New York: Garland, 1991).

2. *Cantates françoises de M. Batistin, livre second* (Paris: Christophe Ballard, 1708), 31–40. For a facsimile edition, see Jean-Baptiste Stuck (Battistin), *Cantatas,* ed. David Tunley, Eighteenth-Century French Cantata, vol. 4 (New York: Garland, 1990), 139–48. Stuck's collection is also available online at http://culture.besancon.fr/ark:/48565/a011307145822j1Jzom.

3. Both settings and their sources are discussed in detail and are presented in modern edition in Kaneez M. Munjee, "*Les chants d'Orphée:* The Figure of Orpheus in the Eighteenth-Century French Cantata" (Ph.D. diss., Stanford University, 2011), 64–66, 74–75, 337, 342, 367–75, 428–42. Guido's setting was published in installments in the December 1710, January 1711, and February 1711 issues of *Recueil d'airs sérieux et à boire* (Amsterdam: Estienne Roger). The December 1710 issue, containing the first three movements, is lost; subsequent movements appear on pp. 1–10 of the January 1711 issue and pp. 31–33 of the February 1711 issue. Lacroix's cantata survives in manuscript in the Bibliothèque municipale de Toulouse, Cons. 918 (7), which is available online at http://numerique.bibliotheque.toulouse.fr/ark:/74899/B315556101_CONS0918_7.

4. No setting of this *Dom Quichote* text is included in the list of surviving cantatas by composers with last names beginning with *B* listed in David Tunley, *The Eighteenth-Century French Cantata,* 2nd ed. (Oxford: Clarendon Press, 1997), 218–26.

5. *Recueil d'airs sérieux,* March 1711, 65–96; April 1711, 95–106. An exemplar is available at The British Library, shelfmark Music Collections C.405.c. I am grateful to Kaneez Munjee for informing me about this setting.

6. Bourgeois's first book of *Cantates françoises* dates from 1708; his second book, *Cantates françoises ou musique de chambre,* dates from 1715 and was reprinted in 1718. He was also successful as both a singer and a composer at the Paris Opéra, producing the *opéra-ballets Les amours déguisés* in 1713 and *Les plaisirs de la paix* in 1715. See the articles from *The New Grove Dictionary of Music and Musicians* and *The New Grove Dictionary of Opera* at *Grove Music Online,* Oxford Music Online (http://www.oxfordmusiconline.com), s.v. "Bourgeois, Thomas-Louis," by David Tunley and Jérôme de La Gorce, respectively. See also Tunley, *Eighteenth-Century French Cantata,* 109–12 and 222–23. I am grateful to Kaneez Munjee for a fruitful e-mail correspondence on this matter.

8277